Free Font Index 3

Hans Lijklema

THE PEPIN PRESS

For my girls

Edited and compiled by Hans Lijklema
All text written by Hans and Karolina Lijklema
English text editing by Rosalind Horton

Cover and book design by Hans Lijklema
lijklema.waw.pl

The typeface Unibody 8 (see pages 257–260) used on the cover was designed by Underware (see pages 29–32). underware.nl
All text set in Anivers, designed by Jos Buivenga of Exljbris. exljbris.com

Free Font Index 3
ISBN 978 90 5768 166 0
The Pepin Press | Agile Rabbit Editions
Amsterdam & Singapore

The Pepin Press BV
P.O. Box 10349
1001 EH Amsterdam
The Netherlands

Tel +31 20 4202021
Fax +31 20 4201152
mail@pepinpress.com
pepinpress.com

10 9 8 7 6 5 4 3 2 1
2018 17 16 15 14 13 12

Manufactured in Singapore

Contents

Introduction

You are holding in your hands the third volume of the *Free Font Index*. I am amazed at the ever-expanding number of free fonts. This area of font distribution has been evolving constantly ever since the publication of the first *Free Font Index* book. Recently, the increasing need for better fonts to be available to designers and the viewers of websites has triggered a whole avalanche of screen fonts, made possible by new developments on the front of web typography. Web designers no longer have to struggle with the small number of system fonts available on every computer, but can now rely on typefaces like Exo (see pages 169–174), which have fonts that are optimised for use on screen. This significantly improves the typographic palette of web designers. Although there is no generally accepted standard at the moment, it is certainly an area that designers as well as companies like Google (see pages 9–12) are working on. Next to the commercial print

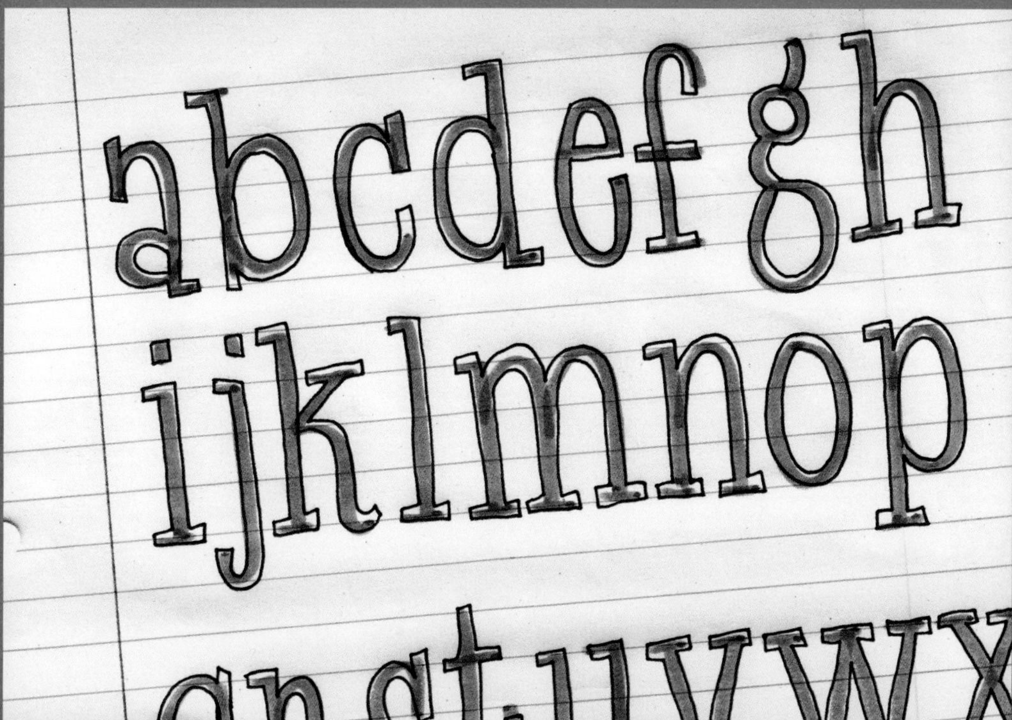

fonts that are acquiring their web companions, a lot of new free high-quality web fonts are starting to appear. There are many designers who are passionate about these new developments and want to improve design standards on the web, like The League of Moveable Type (see pages 155–162 and *Free Font Index 2*, pages 31–38 and 175–182) and Wojciech Kalinowski (see pages 17–20 and 269–282). Some of these designers are able to raise funds through channels such as Kickstarter, which allows them to spend the time they need to perfect their creations. So although they give their fonts away for free, they are rewarded for their design work.

What does all this have to do with the *Free Font Index*, in which we showcase printed type specimens, you ask? What most designers are unaware of is that many of these new free fonts are useable for print design as well. Often these fonts are made available under the OFL (Open Font License). This licence gives much more freedom to the end user than many other free font and commercial font licences. For example, you are allowed to modify and re-distribute these typefaces. Although the advantages of the OFL are most obvious for improving the standards in web design, the licence also makes sense for a lot of graphic designers working with print. While there are excellent free fonts out there, as most of you know, the majority of them have issues like incomplete character sets and need some tweaking. This doesn't prevent their use by professional designers, but it does make it necessary for them to improve the design if they want to use it for more than just a logo or an occasional headline. Of course, anyone can go and buy a commercial font that's technically perfect, but sometimes you find a free font with a nice design concept that you would love to use, not just because it's free.

The OFL also opens possibilities for collaborative typeface design, which is ideal when the original designer is reluctant to expand a typeface. Why not allow other designers to do it? The typeface is improved and the OFL licence guarantees that the modified version will also be available free of charge under the same licence. Collaboration is certainly a big part of the future of typeface design, as the number of languages being covered by OpenType fonts can be daunting. This makes it necessary to consult and collaborate with designers in other parts of the world, because it is often difficult for the original designer of a font to create all possible glyphs, as he or she might not be familiar with all the typographic and linguistic rules that are involved with making non-Latin scripts.

Collaboration is also a great way for design students to learn how to design type. A good example of collaborative type design is the Titillium font family that is being designed by students from the School of Fine Arts in Urbino, Italy. The typeface even spawned an extended version by renowned type designer Chank Diesel. He decided to add italics and additional weights, and also made an alternative upright version to his own liking. He in turn re-released the resulting Panefresco font family under the OFL (see pages 80–86).

Exciting times!

Hans Lijklema

Previous page: sketches for the typeface Believe In Me (see page 196). © 2012 Jakob Fischer | Pizzadude
Opposite: design process of the typeface Rosa (see page 70). © 2012 Ewen Prigent | La Boîte Graphique

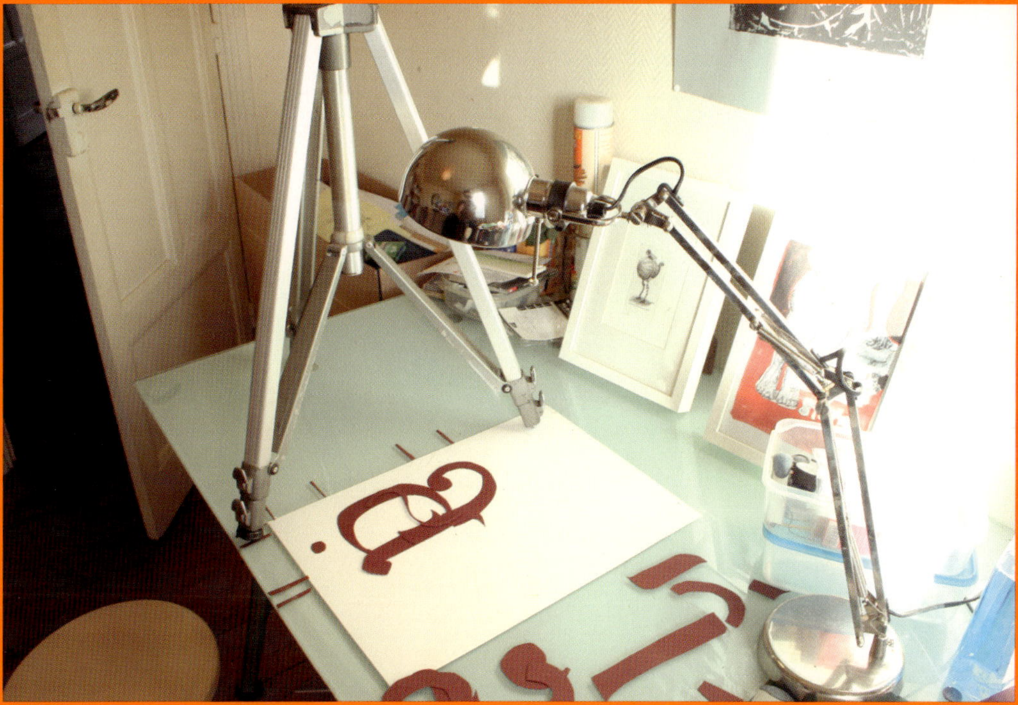

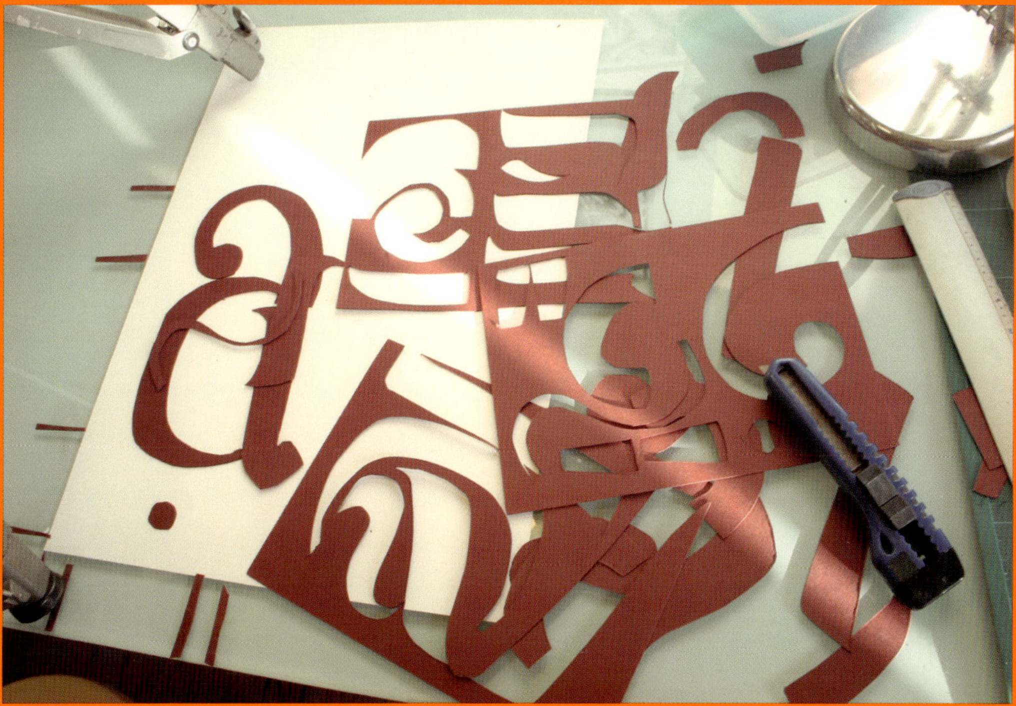

Dave Crossland

Dave Crossland holds an MA degree in Typeface Design from the University of Reading, UK. He has been involved in the libre software movement for a number of years, with a focus on libre fonts. Crossland's Cantarell font family, created as his graduation project, was included in the initial launch of Google Web Fonts in May 2010. Since 2011, Crossland has been a consultant for Google helping them to expand their ever-growing Google Web Fonts library.

You're a big promotor of libre software and especially libre fonts. Should type designers give their fonts away for free and is that for you connected to some kind of mission – design or otherwise?

Dave Crossland: You know, I don't much like the term 'mission', because for me it seems to suggest that my work is in some way religious. I don't see it that way. My work is entirely practical. Libre software and libre fonts are about solving an important practical problem faced every day by everyone

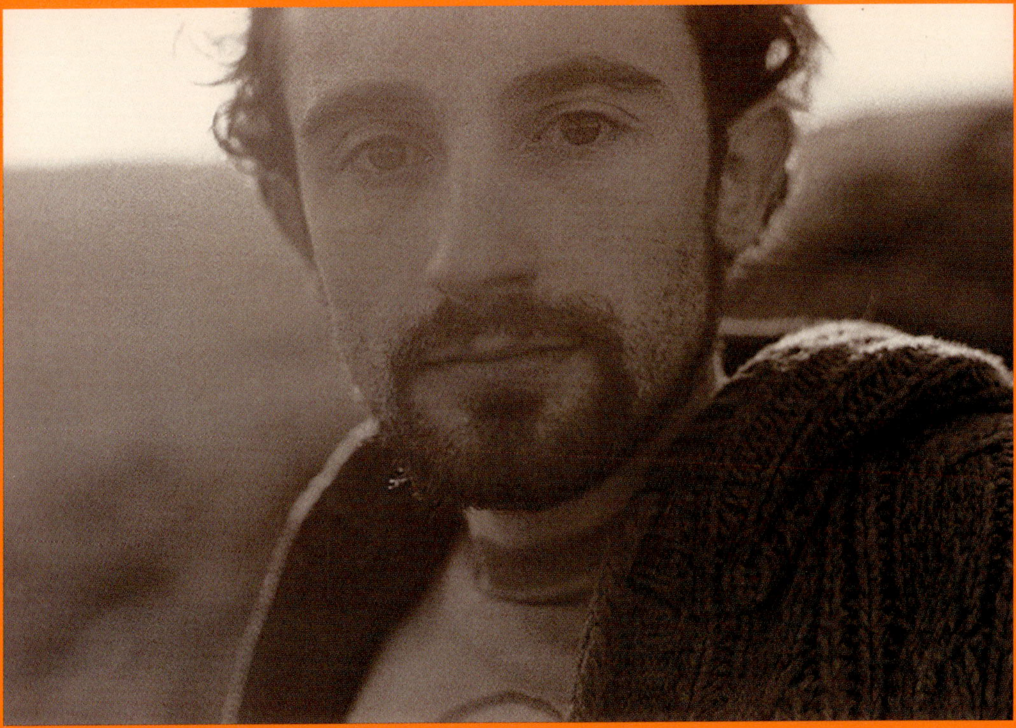

who uses computers. And that means especially people like graphic designers, for whom the use of computers is at the core of what they do. The important issue is – do users have an equal power relation with the designers/developers of their tools? When the initial designers/developers are not interested in fixing an error, do I have the freedom to get someone else to solve the problem? Do I have the freedom to build on their tools, if I find them incomplete for the task at hand? Very often, I found in my design work that I wanted more from my design tools than what was on offer, including fonts. If I want something to be improved, I don't want to be restricted by someone else's lower standards. What I actively promote is the importance of seeking your own freedom, and respecting other designers' freedom. So if a designer is going to make a font available 'for free', gratis, I think making it libre is important too. If a designer is going to sell a font, I think selling it under a libre licence is also important. Business is important, but it is secondary to freedom. I feel this approach has worked well for me.
I don't recommend giving fonts away gratis as a principle – the opposite in fact. All designers should be paid for their work, and that includes designing typefaces. Of course, many people like to design fonts for fun, and I have no problem with that. But it's not something I actively promote.

What came first, the software side or your passion for type and at what point did you decide to combine the two?
Crossland: I loved computers from the day my father bought one, when I was about seven years old. My mother wasn't actually very happy with his purchase, because she knew me and was sure that I'd become addicted! My high school was big enough to have a hacking scene – a group of kids who were totally fascinated with computers and wanted to learn everything about them. Libre software was obviously a big attraction for us. At school I decided to switch my studies from sciences to arts, and then did a one-year Art Foundation diploma at the local art school. There I found typography an interesting mix of the two worlds, and went on to study it at university. At Ravenbourne (formerly Ravenbourne College of Design and Communication), in London, I started to use computers running Mac OS X and the Adobe Creative Suite software. Despite using libre software for many years, I hadn't considered the ethic side of software very deeply. I soon found that I wanted to do things that the proprietary design software did not have features for.
In 2006 I attended the first ever Libre Graphics Meeting and I was very inspired by the potential for libre graphics software to enable new design processes. After graduating that year, I decided that I wanted to make a major contribution to the software freedom movement: I decided to focus on free fonts.
I was very privileged to be accepted into the University of Reading's Masters degree in Typeface Design programme in 2007. I graduated two years later with the typeface design Cantarell (see *Free Font Index 2*, pages 75–78), which became part of the default interface for GNOME 3 – a desktop environment and graphical user interface that runs on top of Unix-like operating systems.

We first crossed paths when you were involved in the Open Font Library (openfontlibrary.org). What has been your role in the project?
Crossland: The Open Font Library has a simple concept: to make it easy for anyone in the world

Opposite, top: Dave Crossland giving a calligraphy demonstration during a workshop at ToyLab in Buenos Aires. Bottom: Dave Crossland conducting a workshop in Córdoba, Argentina. All images © 2012 Christine Cardinal

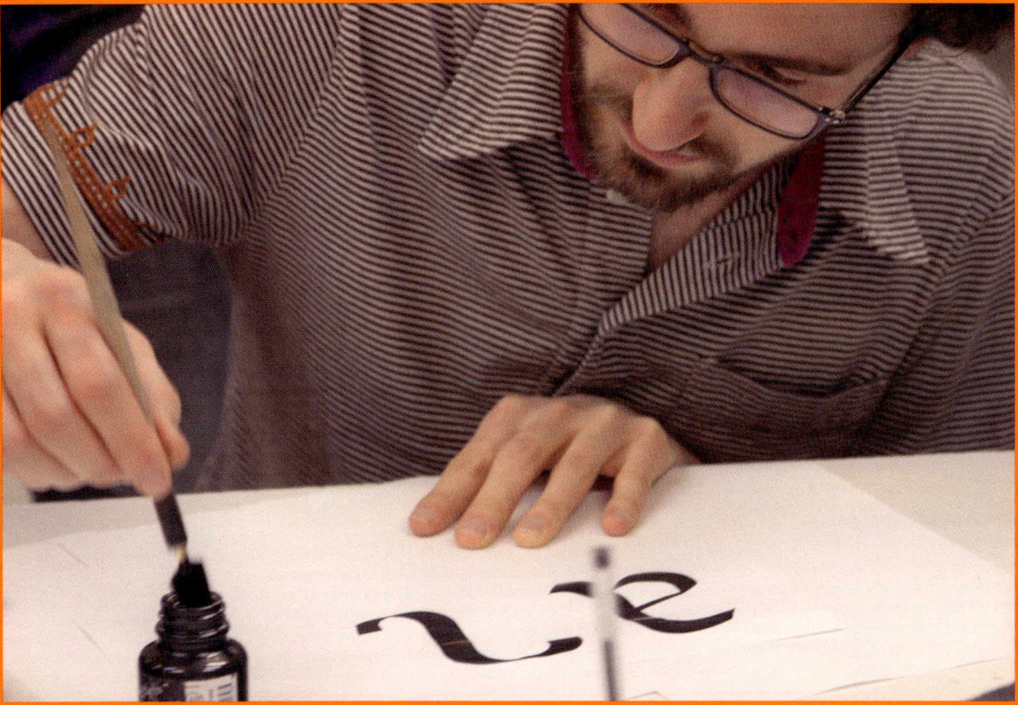

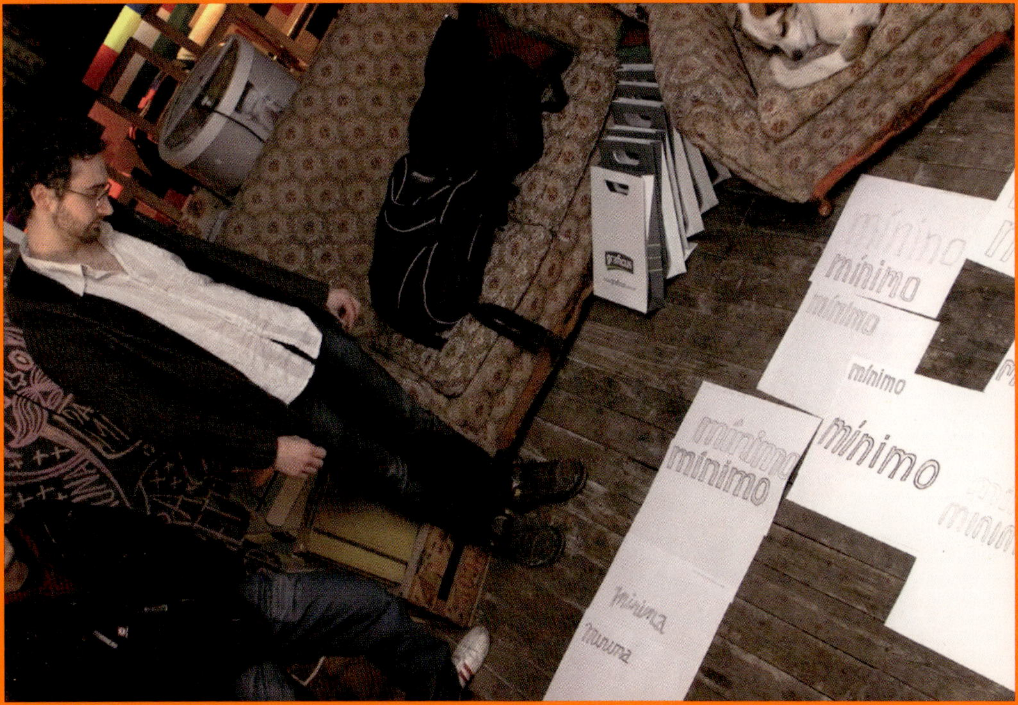
mínimo
mínimo
mínimo
mínimo

to publish a libre font. This means explaining what practical steps are needed to prepare a font as a libre font, and providing an easy way for designers to upload font packages and for users to browse, choose and use the fonts.
I joined the project in 2006, and its progress has been very slow. I've been one of its main promoters, and have funded development on and off over the years, but I have not created a sustainable revenue system. I did some fundraising in 2008 to hire Ben Weiner (see *Free Font Index 1*, pages 213–218) to work on it, as well as Ed Trager. Their work was never fully completed – and I became less involved in the project, partially because I focused on my Masters studies. In 2010 I worked with Pierre Marchand and the OSP design collective, to complete that work on the site, but it still didn't function the way we wanted it to. When the framework we were using for the site was abandoned in 2011, I hired the Fabricatorz, especially Christopher Adams, to work on a totally new site. The initial version was launched at the Libre Graphics Meeting in May 2011. After that I hired the Portuguese designers Manufactura Independente (who coproduce the Libre Graphics Magazine) to further develop the site with Fabricatorz. After the design work was finished, the Fabricatorz team moved it forward in their spare time, completing it in April 2012.

What is it exactly that you do for the Google Web Fonts (google.com/webfonts) project?
Crossland: I work as a consultant to help type designers propose web font projects to the team. While some of the fonts in the Google Web Fonts library are donated, as with the Open Font Library, most of them are created after Google gives the designers financial support to do the design work. I also do technical work to bring the fonts into the system, and I provide advice to the Google Web Fonts team on the overall topic of libre fonts.

You're a frequent lecturer and provide workshops on type design and libre fonts. How did that come about and what do you aim to achieve?
Crossland: In May 2010 I was visiting Brussels for the few weeks leading up to the Libre Graphics Meeting there, and I was invited to give a lecture and workshop at a local design school. It went really badly, which was entirely my own fault. I had never run a workshop before and I felt nervous, and didn't eat or sleep too well the day before. I ended up feeling pretty ill on the day. I stopped it half way through. Awful. So after that, I wasn't very confident about the whole thing. But two type designers living in Brussels, Ludi Loiseau and Seb Sanfilippo, and designer-developer Pierre Marchand, proposed a collaborative type design workshop during the Libre Graphics Meeting. We discussed some ideas for how collaboration could work in type design. We ran with it, and it was a real success! Then a few weeks later I repeated the workshop in Porto, Portugal, with the same result. Since then I've been putting on these events pretty regularly, and varying the format a lot and keeping the things that work best.
I do this because I want to get the idea out that libre fonts are now widely available for people to modify, and that this is a huge new opportunity for designers. Libre culture is a foreign topic for most of them, and I think it's best understood by discussing it in person. So it seemed to me that the best way that I could meet and discuss this with a lot of designers would be to hold lectures and workshops about it.

Disclaimer: Please note that the statements in this interview reflect the personal opinion of Dave Crossland only, and do not represent the views of any other persons, groups or companies.

Paul D. Hunt

Paul Hunt's type design career began with an internship at the P22 Type Foundry, where he both designed his own typefaces and helped to digitise and extend designs created by others. While studying Typeface Design at the University of Reading, he flirted with free fonts, designing several modular fonts (see pages 187–194) using fontstuct.com. After receiving his MA, Hunt landed his current job working for Adobe Systems.

How did you get started in type design?
Paul Hunt: I first began thinking about type design during my undergraduate years. I was hanging out with some guys one night and one said he had made his own font and was using it for his essays. Before that I hadn't really thought about what would be involved in making type. A year or so later, I was looking for some Cyrillic fonts on free font sites, but all the ones I found were not properly encoded. So I started playing with the

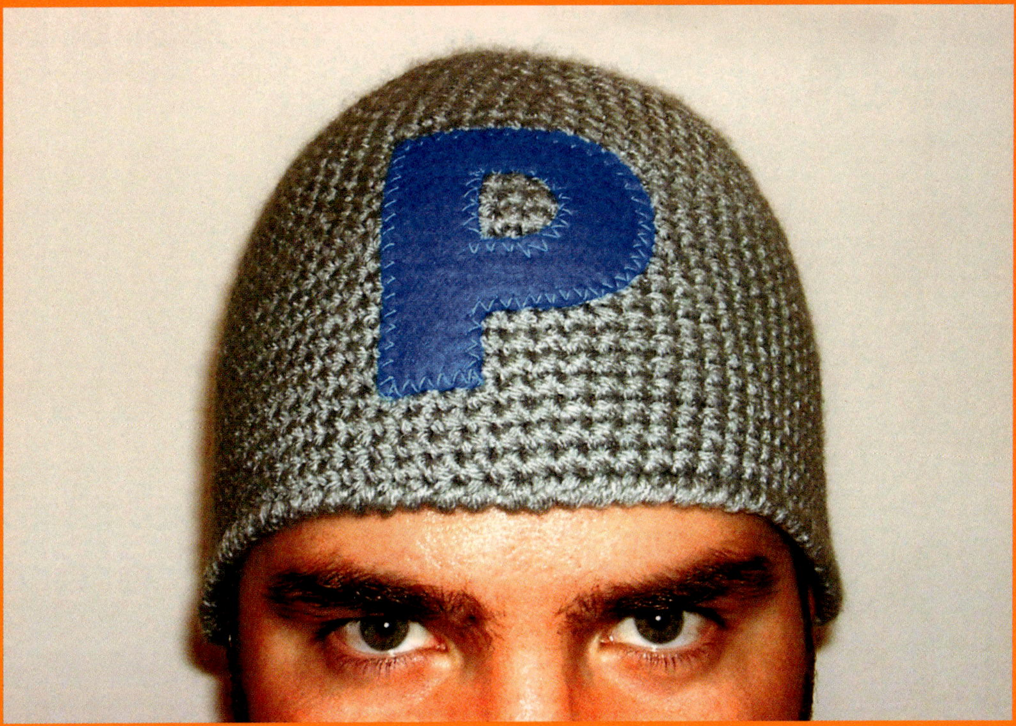

free version of High-Logic's Font Creator software. Eventually I got tired of trying to draw with quadratic splines, and went on eBay to find a used copy of Fontographer. In the meantime I had become addicted to the forums on typophile.com and had started trying to pick the brains of its contributors about how to produce type properly. It was at this point that my type education began in earnest.
I started to read every book on type, lettering and typography that I could lay my hands on. I tried my hand at digitising and drawing a few things, but never got too far, except that I had become fascinated with the capabilities of OpenType and the potential of its layout tables to transform text. With a good deal of help from the experts on Typophile, like Adam Twardoch and John Hudson, I was able to figure out the basics of how to program OpenType features. With this skill under my belt, I was accepted by Richard Kegler, of P22, for what was supposed to be a brief internship to start converting a portion of their newly-acquired Lanston Type font catalogue to feature-rich OpenType. This gig lasted for three years, during which I tried to soak up as much knowledge as I could about type design, font development and non-Latin scripts. After three years, I felt that I wanted to take my design skills to the next level, and being interested in developing type for non-Latin scripts, I decided that the Reading University programme was what I wanted to pursue. This was most definitely the right choice for me to make at that time, because it ultimately led to my landing a job with Adobe. My job at Adobe is a continuation of what I was doing at P22. It involves the production side of font development as well as the design aspect of typeface design. I have been involved in projects developing OpenType features for Hebrew and Arabic fonts, and I have been designing Adobe's first-ever open source font family under the direction of the eminent Robert Slimbach.

When you're drawing a new typeface, are you inspired by type history, contemporaries or things outside the field of type design?
Hunt: In terms of inspiration, I'd say I take cues from many different sources. I do love old specimen books and have probably spent days of my life poring over them. I'm always craning my neck to catch sight of some bit of interesting lettering or stopping to document things by taking a photo. Or sometimes I'll see some design element that resonates with me but that I have not seen realised in a typeface. But most frequently, I am just given a brief and have to develop a typeface according to parameters that have been set.

You are clearly inspired by the multilingual aspect of type design. Where do you find the drive to work on concepts with such huge amounts of glyphs?
Hunt: I have always been interested in other languages and cultures as well as design. It seems to me that type is a logical intersection of these two interests. I studied Russian language in junior high and high school and at university level, which introduced me to reading and writing a new script. It was only natural to experiment with developing Cyrillics for some of the font projects I worked on at P22.
In the past I have been driven to develop such large glyph sets for another reason as well: I am enamoured by alternative glyphs. I like to see how the overall flavour of a typeface can be changed by modifying the details to a handful of glyphs. For example, in the P22 Underground Pro project that I completed, I just had to see what Edward Johnston's letters would look like if all of his ingenious alternative glyphs were made

Opposite: sketches and test prints made for typefaces designed while studying at the University of Reading. All images © 2012 Paul D. Hunt

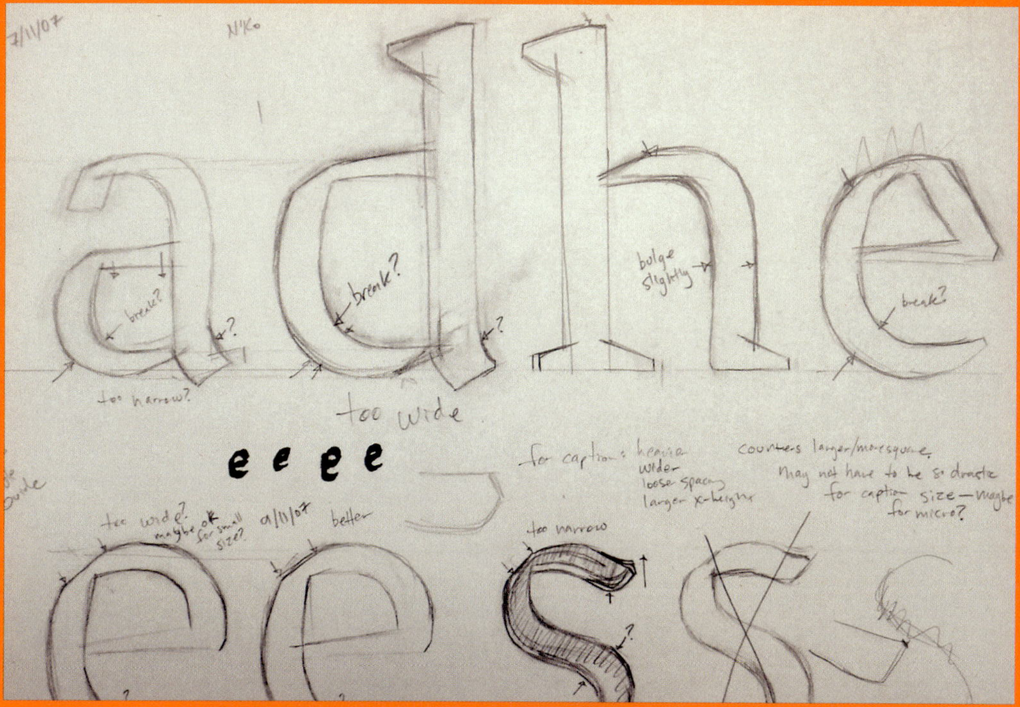
adhe
too narrow?
break?
too wide
bulge slightly
for caption: heavier
wider
loose spacing
larger x-height
counters larger/more square
May not have to be so drastic
for caption size—maybe
for micro?
better
too narrow

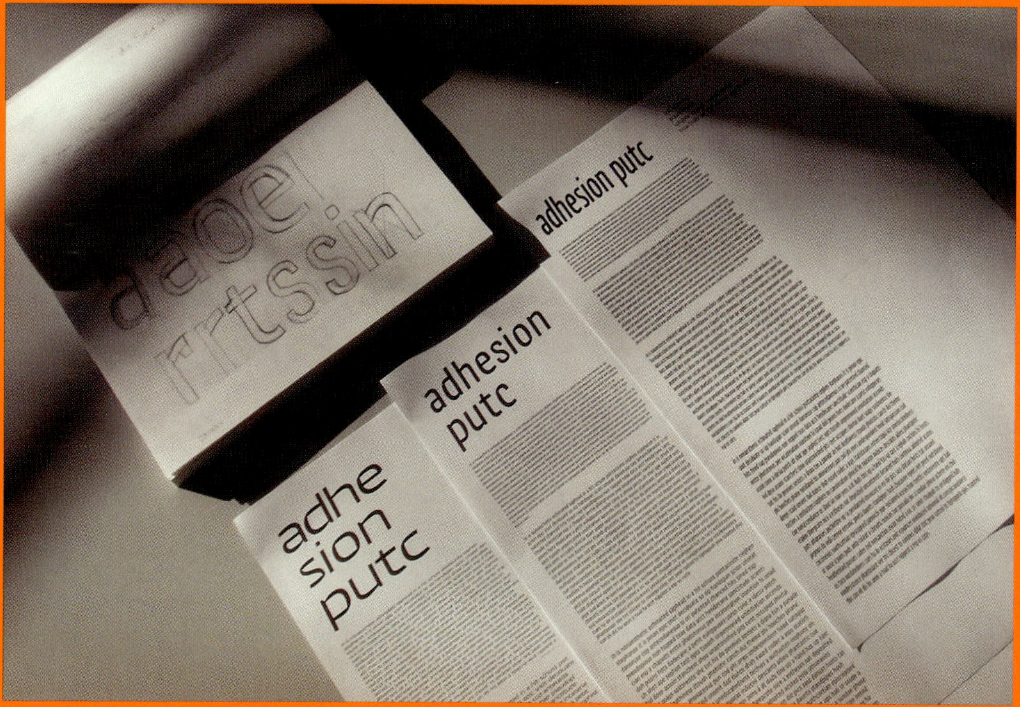
adhesion putc
adhesion
putc
adhe
sion
putc

available. I also wanted to give users the option to change the very distinctive diamond-shaped dots for more traditional round ones. And I also made some geometric alternatives for glyphs like *a* and *g*. On top of that, of course, I wanted to add Greek and Cyrillic support. Not just simple support, but support for polytonic Greek and minority languages that use Cyrillic script.

In your opinion, why does it still make sense to come up with new fonts, when there are already so many out there?
Hunt: On one hand, a typeface is a design and as such is sometimes categorised in terms of art or fashion: we need new typefaces that fit with the visual culture of our time. On the other hand, much of the most important design work is developed as a response to real practical needs. For so long much of the body of type available on the market was focused solely on the medium of print. More and more, type is moving to screen-based media. The fonts that were developed with old media in mind are not always appropriate for the new media. Technology will continue to change, thanks to which there will be new demands and requirements for design solutions to address these changes. So as long as the design of a typeface is married to the technology of fonts, there will always be the need for these crucial components of visual communication to adapt to the changes we see in society and in technology.

You joined FontStruct (see Free Font Index 1, pages 21–23) in 2008, not long after its release. What got you hooked? It's quite different from the script fonts you were designing at P22.
Hunt: I got hooked on FontStruct during my year at Reading. I think in a way I used it as a tool to take a simple concept for a typeface design and apply the design parameters consistently across the whole range of characters that I would design for each type style. So in a way, it was part of my education that year. For me, it was something quick, fun and instructive to build fonts from modular parts. Because I consider the results to be of somewhat limited use, I decided to make them freely available for others to use and remix.

How do you feel free fonts influence the pay fonts market?
Hunt: From my perspective, free fonts are typically a benefit to the paid font industry as they increase the awareness of type and typography among the general public, creating more potential customers and clients. However, my feeling is that for anyone genuinely interested in design, the majority of free fonts available will rarely be adequate either in terms of design or in terms of technical reliability. Part of my own education in typeface design was born out of a desire to improve the quality of certain free fonts in certain ways: to add missing glyphs or to properly encode characters. Not all font users will have the inclination to do this. So in my personal experience, free fonts were a gateway to exposing me to the importance of good typography and, as I increased my type knowledge, I began to recognise the difference in quality of various free fonts. I also began to notice that more of the well-made fonts that I was interested in were only available with a paid licence. Eventually I stopped evaluating and using fonts on the basis of monetary cost and judged them more in terms of design quality. I still find good free fonts from time to time. I consider this a real treat whenever it happens.

Wojciech Kalinowski

Wojciech Kalinowski has a different background from most people designing typefaces. His daily work in stonemasonry as a carver of inscriptions fuelled his interest in typography and type design, leading him (as WMK69) to release his own digital fonts. Kalinowski's preference for traditional draftsmanship is evident in many of his typefaces. His fonts, which are all part of the Open Font Library, are a wonderful combination of the physical and the virtual.

At what point in your life did you become interested in letters?

Wojciech Kalinowski: Actually, everything for me started with sculpting. From an early age I sculpted in clay. Like most children I could spend hours on end creating all kinds of things from modelling clay. I was always more interested in sculptures than letters, but I liked old Gothic inscriptions too. I was born in Wrocław (Poland), where I still live. This is an old city with a long history and many historic

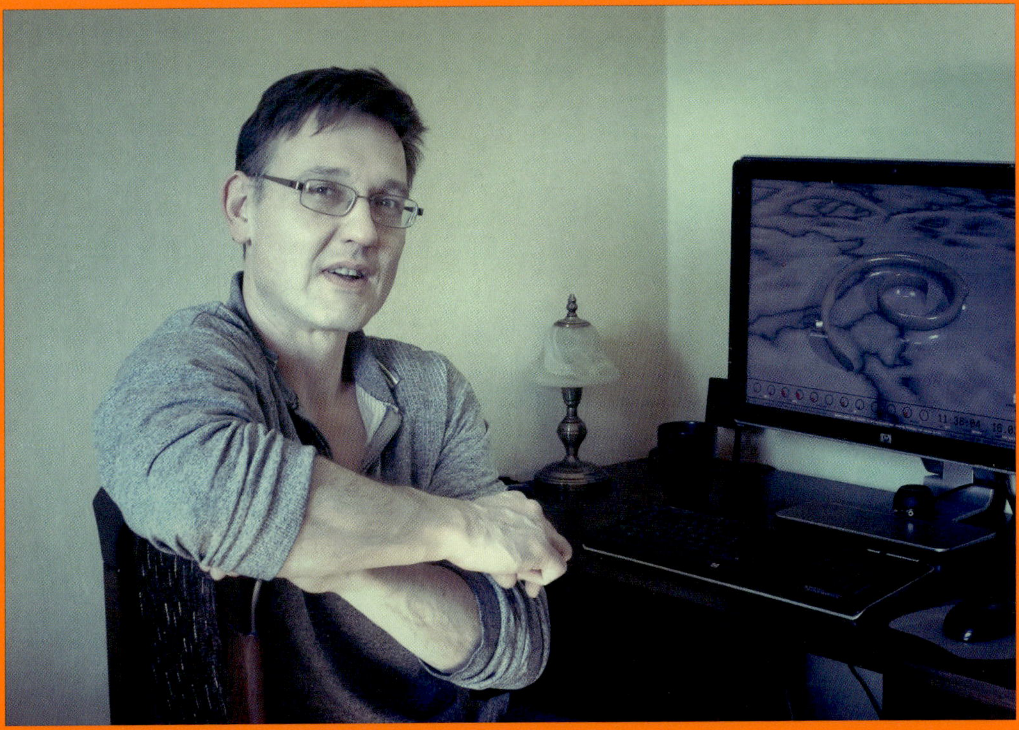

churches and buildings. I always liked to look at them and study the reliefs and old inscriptions in stone, but I didn't think about stonemasonry or similar professions at that stage.
I began working as a stonemason in 1990. In those days everything was done manually. Letters were first drawn directly on stone and then carved by hand. Almost everyone who made inscriptions in stone did simple, squared letters with slightly rounded corners. It was easy and fast. In the beginning I did the same, but I wasn't entirely happy with the results. I began improving my letters, adding more rounded corners, serifs and sharp endings to the letters – something like Roman Square Capitals. Part of the improvements was the result of studying the work of other people who made inscriptions. After a few years I designed my first typeface – Modern Antiqua. Next I made Medieval Sharp and Gothica – both based on old Gothic inscriptions – and Cursive Serif – a decorative, italic typeface. I still use these typefaces today in my own work and I always draw them by hand.

How important is history to you and for your type designs? You mentioned that you are inspired by old inscriptions, but does print have an influence on you as well?

Kalinowski: I think that history is important for everybody. It reminds us of who we are and where we came from, and teaches us how to avoid repeating mistakes from the past.
I like to take concepts from the past and I never made any distinction between inscriptions in stone and print. Some of my typefaces are inspired by inscriptions in stone, and others by printed typographic works like old prints and books. If I see something I like, I try to put a spin on it and make it mine. I don't like to copy anything 'as is'. I wouldn't, for example, like to make an exact revival of an old metal typeface. Sometimes the final effect is something totally different from what I was expecting when I started.

Did any of your fonts develop from your stone carvings?

Kalinowski: Yes, typefaces like Modern Antiqua, Medieval Sharp, Gothica and Cursive Serif, that I mentioned before, were all digitised. I designed all of these alphabets in the second half of the '90s for my stone carving work. Originally they consisted only of uppercase letters and digits, except for Cursive Serif – which was the first full alphabet I drew. A few years ago I drew the missing lowercase letters for several alphabets, and I tried to do it digitally. For the occasion I expanded some of the existing designs by adding new weights or styles. For example, I added Cursive Sans to Cursive Serif, and the Nova family was based on my unpublished font Gothica. There is also Classica, based on Roman Square Capitals, but it is totally different from the one I use for my work.

Are you able to use your typefaces in your stone carving work?

Kalinowski: My clients invariably choose the font Modern Antiqua. Sometimes I get to use Medieval Sharp, or Cursive Serif, but that's all. For the majority of clients, my more recent typeface designs are too modern looking to be used for inscriptions in stone. Ninety-nine per cent of my work consists of inscriptions and reliefs on gravestones. Sometimes I do commemorative plaques for churches or public institutions. All very serious stuff. They must have a traditional look, so there is very little room to play.
Designing a typeface is my way of expressing

Opposite: examples of hand stone carving for different gravestones. All images © 2012 Wojciech Kalinowski

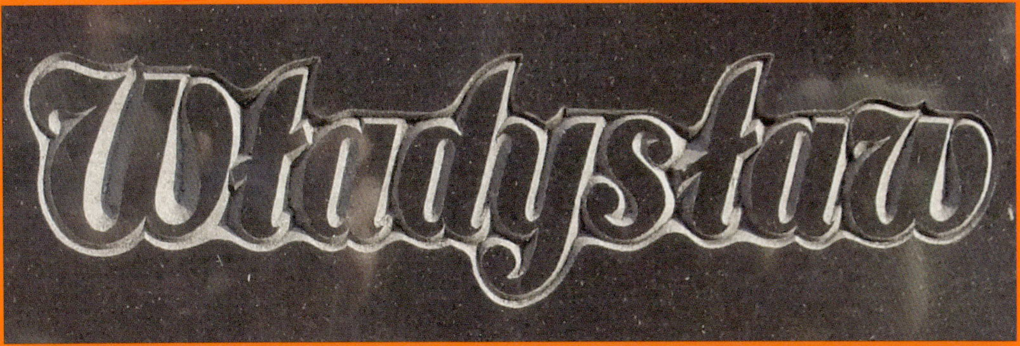
Władysław

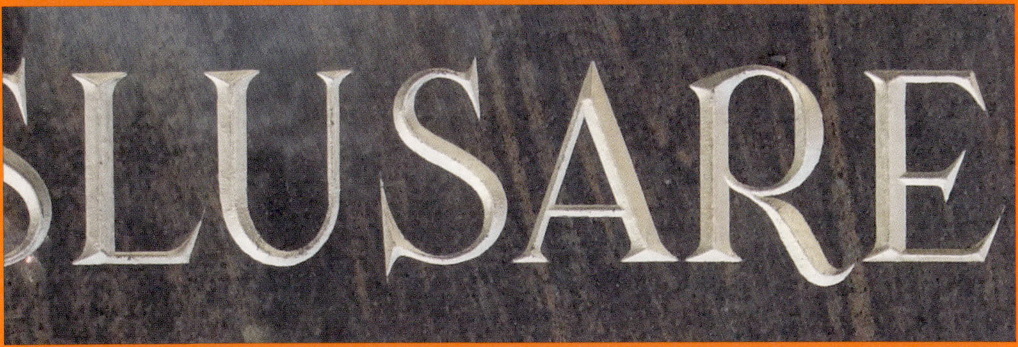
SLUSARE

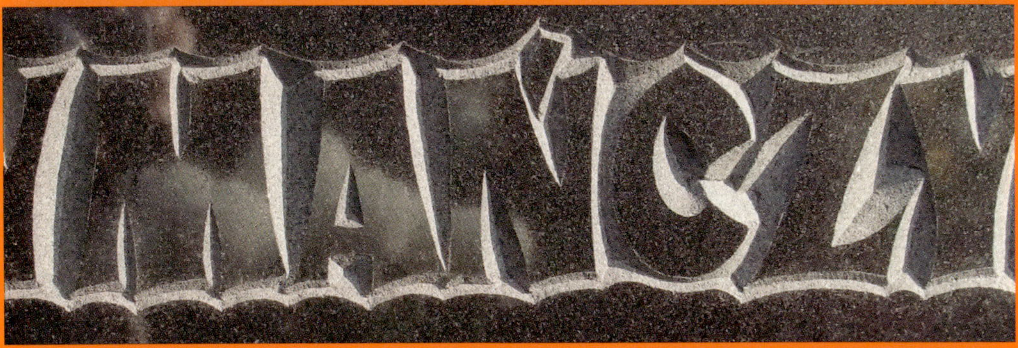

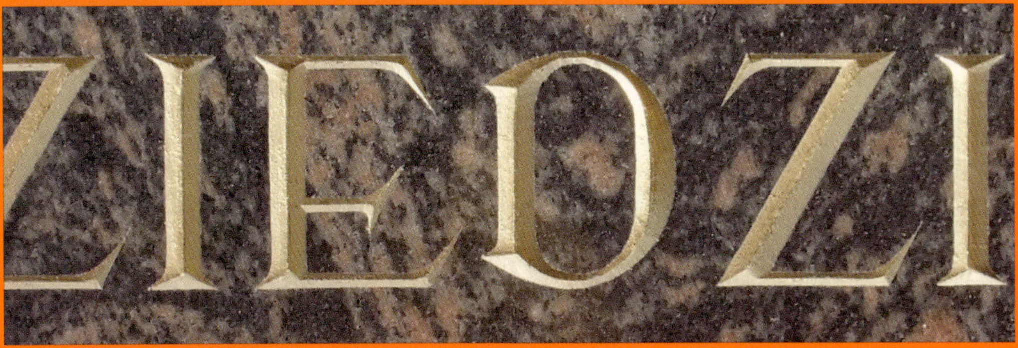

myself. Every time I begin to create a new font, I try to do something unique. When I create digital fonts I feel free. Sometimes I'm able to use my ideas in my professional work, but generally I have to do what my clients want.

What made you decide to digitise your alphabets, that you used for hand carving, and create fonts out of them?

Kalinowski: At one point I became interested in Linux, an open source operating system, of which the desktop is fully customisable. You can change everything: wallpapers, window themes, icons, cursors and fonts. I played around with all those things, but I missed nice fonts with Polish glyphs. Most free fonts contain only the basic set of Latin glyphs used in most western European languages, but as I live in Poland, that wasn't sufficient for my needs. I began to add Polish letters to existing fonts, and that taught me something about creating digital fonts. Then I thought about digitising my own typefaces, so I began by first scanning my old alphabets. Later I tried my hand at designing new typefaces, using all my ideas that I had never had the opportunity to carve in stone. My first trials weren't as good as I wanted them to be and I had to redesign them. There are some quite large differences between drawing letters on paper or stone and creating a digital font. Generally, the alphabets I use for my work are not useable as digital fonts. For example, when I draw the sharp ends of letters and serifs it looks very good in stone, but scaling these details down on the computer or in print makes them look too fragile. This is the reason why digital fonts have their serifs and the sharp ends of the letters constructed differently. That's also the reason why most digital fonts are unusable for carving in stone without modifying them a little. This is only one of many differences, and it's really hard to mention all of them. Designing each digital alphabet brings about new problems and new questions, and every one of them must be dealt with individually.

Why did you decide to release your typefaces under the OFL licence, and what were you hoping to achieve?

Kalinowski: As I just mentioned, I had become interested in Linux, which in turn also sparked my curiosity in the open source software movement. I thought this was a great idea, and I wanted to be part of it. I decided to contribute by making my typefaces open and free. I hoped that it would increase the number of free fonts with Polish glyphs! I really didn't expect anything in return. Sometimes I receive a mail with nice words, like: 'Good work. Thanks!'. It stimulates me to do this work more than money ever could. Like your invitation to be a part of this book.
I'm not considering releasing commercial fonts now, or in the future. I want my fonts to remain open and free. We are living in a world dominated by money, and we often forget that we can do something for free, and be happy because of it. I try to remind other people of that. Try it! It really doesn't hurt!

Wouldn't you like to move out of stone carving and more into type design?

Kalinowski: Totally move out of it? I hope I'll never have to. I like to work with stone, as well as to design type digitally. I might, however, be forced to move out of stone carving at some point. Each year there are fewer orders for my work. I make inscriptions the traditional way – I still draw all letters out by hand and later carve them in stone with a chisel and hammer or pneumatic hammer. Nowadays this type of work is most often done by computers and all kinds of different machines and techniques to speed up the process.

Santiago Orozco

Santiago Orozco studied Computational Systems Engineering at Monterrey University, Mexico, but his passion for graphic design and typography got the better of him. His extensive Josefin font family (see pages 232–238) is a modern reinterpretation of geometric typefaces from the interwar period – such as Futura, Kabel and Memphis. Orozco works at the Danilo Black design agency, and in the evening runs his own foundry Typemade.

When did your passion for type design start?
Santiago Orozco: Well, I think it all began when I was a kid. From the moment my mother bought me some Letraset sheets and stencil letter templates. I recall spending hours drawing letters in my notebooks and books. I remember that when I was about ten years old an advertisement caught my eye, while reading a magazine that my aunt had brought along. More specifically, the typeface that had been used in the ad caught my eye.

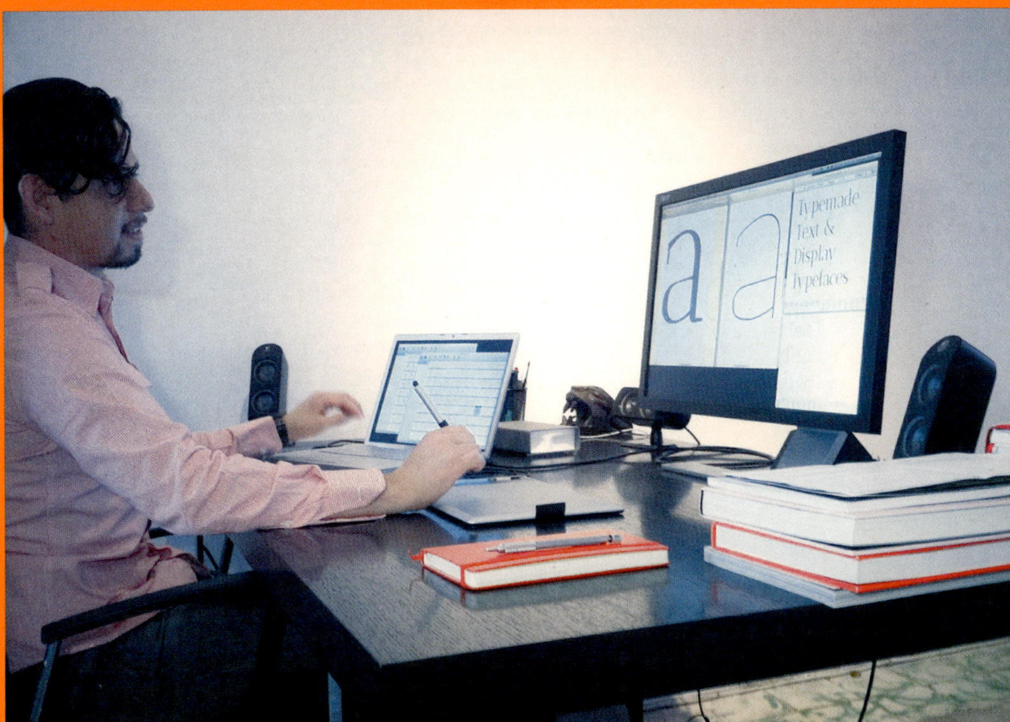

I've always liked everything about graphic design. When I was at high school I wanted to start my own design studio and create nice stuff, like the things I was surrounded with every day. But then I decided to be more practical, or so I thought, and enrolled to study Computational Systems Engineering. While studying engineering I sneaked into all the design classes by talking to the teachers and asking their permission to attend their courses. This way I managed to attend almost all the graphic design courses at the university, as well as some more in art history plus my regular engineering courses.

As a requirement, we had to choose two courses from a different discipline to complement engineering. As I was getting better and better at graphic design, I decided to choose the typography course, and fell in love with it. I also discovered the name of the typeface that I had seen in my aunt's magazine. It turned out to be Rotis, designed by Otl Aicher. As soon as I had completed the typography course I knew that this was what I wanted to do for the rest of my life.

Why did you decide to release such a substantial part of your fonts under the Open Font Licence?

Orozco: After studying typography for five years I decided in 2009 to spread my wings and become a type designer and start my own design studio at the same time. During my studies I had spent a lot of nights reading almost everything I could find about typography and type design – resources available on the internet, as well as books and articles – and finally I started to experiment with calligraphy. I really learned everything on my own. When I started with the design of my first typeface, Josefin, my goal was to explore how to produce large font families.

As it was my first typeface, I didn't think people would be willing to pay for something unfinished or imperfect. I also didn't think my Josefin family would ever have the success it now has. That was quite a surprise! It was part of the initial launch of Google Web Fonts in May 2010, which of course really helped it to become this popular.

Although I still publish new fonts under the OFL licence, lately I have been working on some typefaces that I plan to release as commercial fonts. Some of them are new and a couple are expansions from my free fonts. I hope to build on their current success and, through the sale of these extended versions, to be able to dedicate more of my time to designing type.

Typemade is your own foundry, but as you don't sell any retail fonts at the moment you must have a day job...

Orozco: Yes, I'm working full time as a typographer and information architect at Danilo Black. One of its founders is designer Roger Black, who of course is well known for his involvement with the magazine *Rolling Stone.* The agency works on diverse multimedia projects and I'm responsible for the typography and the architecture of many of the agency's assignments. What I like most about this job is defining and composing blocks of text, exploring the textures created by different typefaces and delivering designs that captivate the readers.

Even though Typemade isn't my day job, it's certainly not a side project. At first, I just wanted to draw beautiful letters that would be used all over the world by the best designers, but now I'm aiming to produce high-quality text and display typefaces for use in magazines and newspapers. As I mentioned before, I'm planning to move more

Opposite, top: sketches for the Josefin Slab font family (see pages 235–238). Bottom: sketches for the typeface Antic (see page 230).

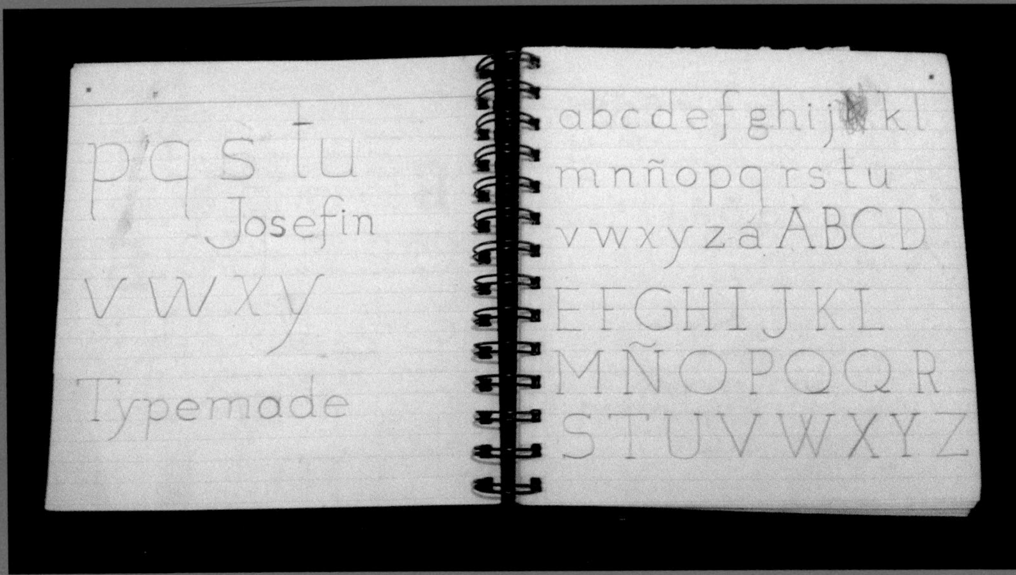
p q s tu
Josefin
v w x y
Typemade
abcdefghijkl
mnñopqrstu
vwxyzá ABCD
EFGHIJKL
MÑOPQQR
STUVWXYZ

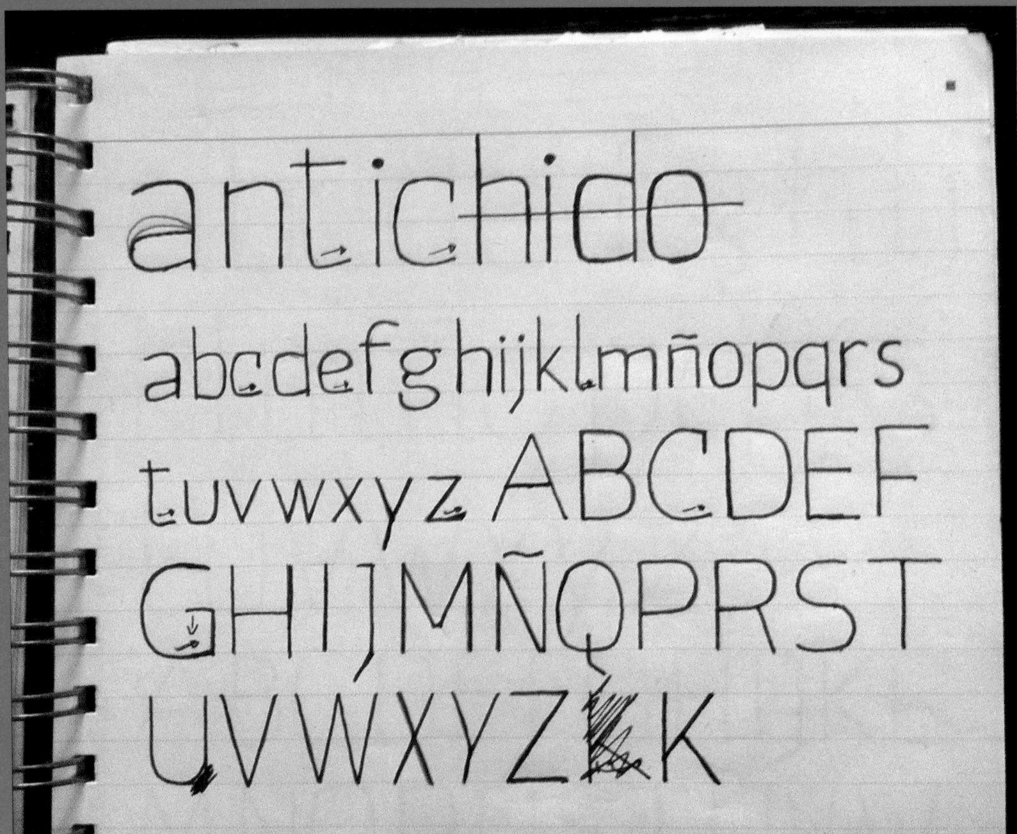
antichido
abcdefghijklmñopqrs
tuvwxyz ABCDEF
GHIJMÑQPRST
UVWXYZK

into the direction of commercial fonts, hoping that at some point I will be able to focus solely on designing typefaces – day and night.

How important is type history for you when you design a typeface and to what extent do you feel your designs are rooted in Mexican or Latin-American culture?
Orozco: I don't think that my typeface designs are greatly influenced by any Latin-American aesthetic, but I am very aware of the beautiful vernacular lettering that surrounds me.
However, type history in general is very important to me! When it comes to the design of a typeface, it's my conviction that every design decision has to be deliberate, and also has to be justified. When designing typefaces, you cannot ignore 500 years of history.
My Josefin typeface was definitely well informed by type history. It's really my own take on several 'geometric' sans serif fonts from the beginning of the last century. My main purpose is to design new and improved typefaces, by learning from others' mistakes and experiments. Type design is an evolutionary discipline. You are always building on the work of the designers who came before you and trying to improve on what they have created as well as discovering something new.

Is there a substantial Mexican type scene? Can you tell me something about that?
Orozco: Yes, there are some good guys out there, and most of them participate in the biennial Tipos Latinos, where designers from all over Latin-America show their work. We also celebrate 'Typographers Day' on 25 September, to commemorate that, in 1537, Juan Cromberger – a printer from Seville – started printing in Mexico. He was the first printer to be established in America – the continent, not the country. Every year the Mexican design community celebrates this event with lectures, workshops and exhibitions.

What inspires you to make a new font?
Orozco: It might sound a bit vague, but for me it all starts with a feeling, and that feeling defines the personality of the typeface. Of course, the feeling that I'm trying to translate into the final design of a typeface originates from its intended use. If it's supposed to be used for running text, it has to be very legible and functional, even at small sizes. If it's a display face I focus more on its visual impact, elegance, modernity, and – most important of all – try to ensure that it will be different and unique.
At the same time the work of other type designers is also a huge inspiration. Maybe not literally, but their designs and work ethic set a kind of standard to work towards. For example, I admire the work of Christian Schwartz. For me he's one of the most talented type designers around at the moment. I'm also big fan of David Berlow, and not just because of his typefaces, but since I started studying typography I've reached many of the same conclusions about our profession as he did, and I also discovered that I have a similar taste in typography. Roger Black, who I mentioned earlier, is also a partner in the renowned foundry Font Bureau, which he founded together with Berlow. It's a small world.
And last but not least, nature is very inspiring to me. I'm fascinated by the patterns that can be found in nature. But no matter what kind of font I produce, I always just try to create beautiful glyphs and ensure that it's technically sound.

Dirk Uhlenbrock

Dirk Uhlenbrock is an award-winning illustrator, graphic designer and type designer, from Essen, Germany. He released his first free fonts under the name Eyesaw, later followed by his Fontomas free font project, which in turn sparked his commercial type foundry TypeType, selling extended versions of his free fonts. Uhlenbrock started his design career at the beginning of the '90s, and is currently creative director at the Erste Liga design agency.

Was Eyesaw really your first font project, or was there anything before?

Dirk Uhlenbrock: Yes, it was my first endeavour in creating digital type. Of course, I have always been interested in type, ever since I got my first Letraset catalogues and sheets when I was ten. I tried to construct and draw letters and also dabbled in calligraphy. I created an alphabet for a computer game before starting Eyesaw, but it was hand drawn and then digitised by a colleague.

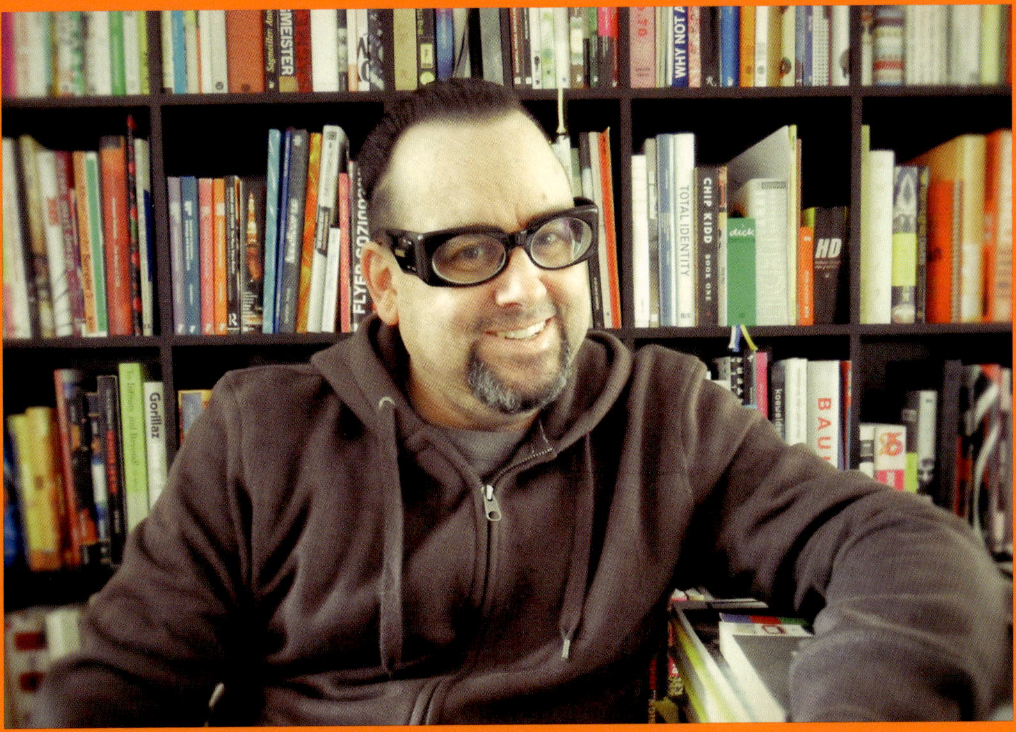

When I started a job as an art director in a multimedia-company I got the chance to work with Fontographer and I was 'electrified' from the first moment. The possibility of creating a 'product' that could be easily distributed was an idea that has never lost its fascination for me. So I started to experiment and when the first 10 to 20 typefaces were done I decided to give them away for free on a website. That's how Eyesaw was born and thanks to word of mouth it reached so many people around the globe that I was motivated to create more fonts. The most fascinating thing for me at that moment was to get in touch with other designers from all over the world, to exchange ideas, to know how they live and the way they work. The daily feedback I received began to shrink after a year online, but the amount of downloads didn't, so I decided to change the way of distribution from a source that is available all the time to a restricted format that provides one font a week for only seven days: and so fontomas.com was born. The goal for me was to have a new font available every week on a Wednesday. Some other designers asked me if they could participate, so I released their fonts too. Of course I received many e-mails from people who had missed a week or who had heard of the project when it was already halfway through. So in the end I decided to collect the fonts on a CD and give the profit I made to charity.

After Fontomas you started your own type foundry called TypeType. Why the change?
Uhlenbrock: I got requests during the Fontomas year to expand some of the free fonts into full alphabets or to add foreign glyphs and accents. Some of my clients saw the fonts and liked them, so they paid me to make a 'pro' version. Thanks to this I was able to spend serious time on developing these typefaces further. At that point I felt that I had acquired enough experience to take it a bit more seriously and to try to sell my typefaces. It has been quiet around TypeType for some time now, because for the most part I'm making my living as a graphic designer. This has taken so much of my time during the last couple of years, that I haven't been able to find a quiet moment to work on the various drafts and concepts for new typefaces I've collected in the meantime. I'm a father of six children and it takes a lot of work to keep such a 'family business' running. But things are getting easier now and I've recently been working on some typefaces. One of the bigger projects is a corporate typeface for a children's bookstore.

Did the popularity of a free font version help to motivate people to buy the extended commercial version of the same font?
Uhlenbrock: I think that someone who wanted to buy a font would find it helpful if they could first try it out – so I feel free versions will always stimulate the sale of the commercial version of a given font. Of course, in the case of the Fontomas fonts, the free versions were no longer available by the time the commercial versions were released. So it's hard to measure if it helped the sales, but it sure helped to get attention for my type designs and other creative work.

You say that you don't consider yourself a type designer, but rather somebody who loves to draw letters. Is it safe to say that you have an illustrative approach to type design and that the glyphs in your fonts are a kind of illustration in themselves?
Uhlenbrock: Yes indeed. I'm an illustrator and I guess that people who draw see things a bit

Opposite, top: package design for the Fontomas font collection CD. Bottom: promotional images for the Fontomas free fonts Pellegrini (see page 250) and Ove (see page 248). All images © 2012 Dirk Uhlenbrock | TypeType

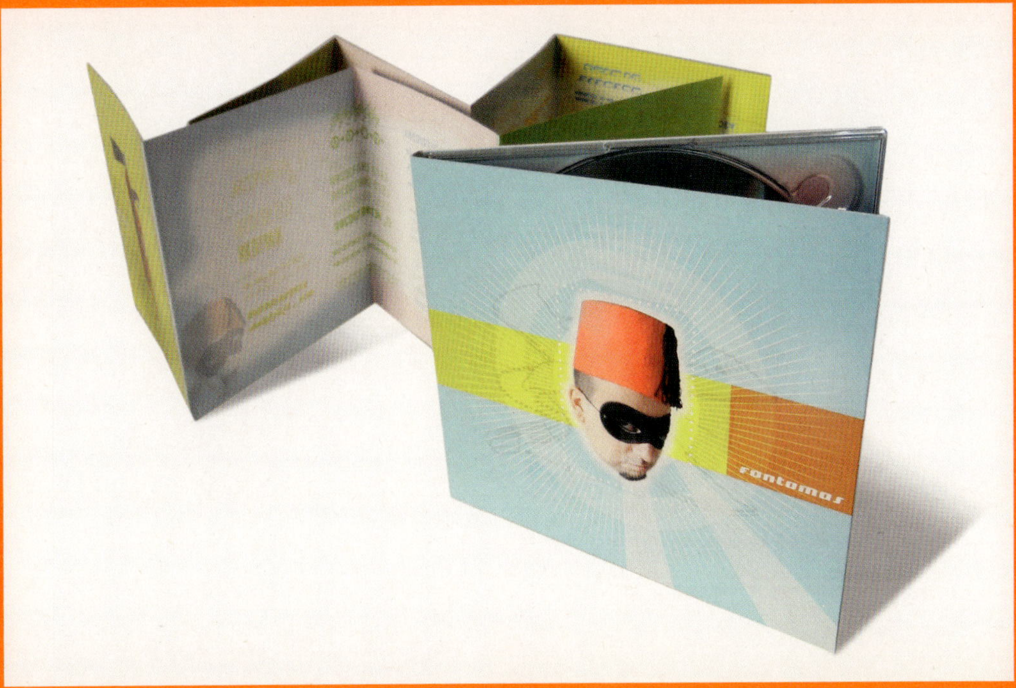
fontomas

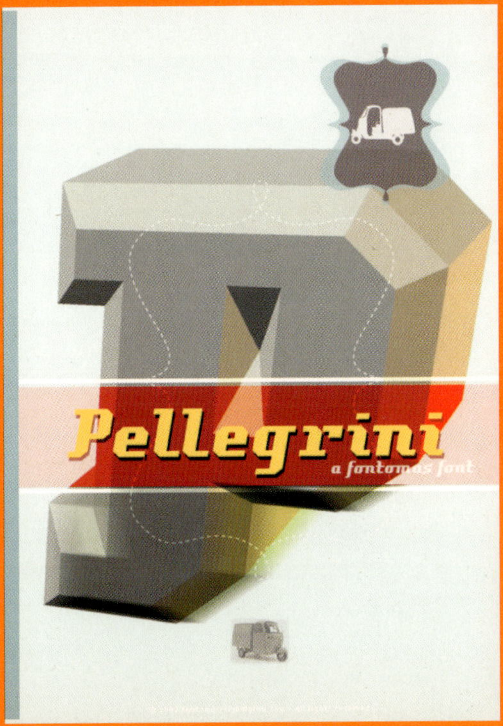
Pellegrini
a fontomas font

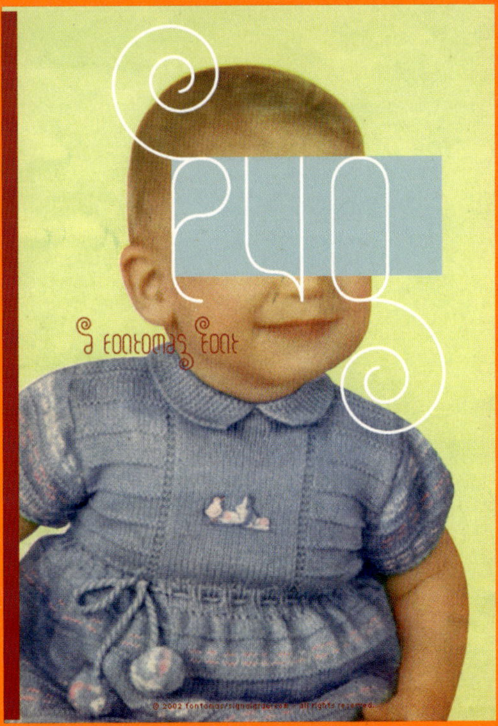
a fontomas font

differently. I treat every single sign or letter as an illustration. I can get really excited about a form or the white space a glyph produces. I'm working with type every day because I create a lot of logos, and when I'm working on one I always feel the urge to alter, optimise, redraw and add on to the shape of a letter. Even when I use existing typefaces. It's something that comes naturally and is stronger than me.

When you design a font, do you keep the end user in mind or is it more your own artistic expression that might be useful for somebody else later on?
Uhlenbrock: No – I've never produced a font with the user in mind. I've always done this for my own enjoyment and will continue to do so. It's more a 'finger exercise' or a kind of meditation for me – not work. Most of the fonts started with just a single idea of a form, inspiration I got from stuff I saw in a publication, on the streets or somewhere else. I start with one character and then I begin to draw other glyphs to see if the idea, the construction of the form, can be applied to the other letters of the alphabet.

Do you sometimes have the feeling that somebody has overused one of your free fonts or used it to communicate messages with which you might not agree?
Uhlenbrock: No. As I mentioned a moment ago, I never consider in which way a font might be used – but I've often been surprised by the context in which some of my typefaces have turned up in advertisements or on packages. However, it's always a fun experience to see what others are doing with them. I've seen my fonts on all kinds of printed matter like cornflakes packaging, flyers, ads and in online use on websites. As I mentioned before, I have expanded some of my free fonts on request for special requirements like a TV-promotion or a headline font for a magazine and it was a pleasure to see that they work properly in their new surrounding. If a typeface fits well, that makes my day. It just makes me happy if someone else has fun working with my fonts.

Is it important for you to see what other designers are up to and is the work of competitors inspiring?
Uhlenbrock: Well, I don't compete with other designers – only with myself. I'm never content with my work and output for very long, which is what keeps me curious and pushes me to try out new things. I guess that's the main issue every single creative has to struggle with. But yes, of course, seeing what others are working on is the fuel that keeps me running. I like to be inspired every day, so I buy a lot of graphic design books and check my online resources on a daily basis.

You started your career in the '90s, at a point when, thanks to technical advancements such as the internet and retail font creation software, it became much easier to do your own thing in type design. Would you have considered designing typefaces if you'd started 10 or 20 years before you did?
Uhlenbrock: It's a fact that the technology helps you a lot to express yourself, and gives you a great deal of freedom. So, I think that I would still have drawn letters, but I'm not sure if I would have gone as far as to try and get one of my designs produced through conventional channels. Certainly free fonts would have been out of the question, of course. If I had had the same conditions back then when I started my design studies as I have now, my career and progress would have been totally different. It's so easy now to self-publish things and to get your work noticed by using the internet and social media – my 'world' or, better, my every-day life experiences have been hugely expanded in 25 years.

Underware

Underware is an international type design collective, founded by Akiem Helmling, Bas Jacobs and Sami Kortemäki. They are currently based in The Hague, Amsterdam and Helsinki respectively and are best known for typefaces like Dolly, Sauna, Liza, Bello and Fakir. The collective also designed the logo for MyFonts, they are cofounders of Typeradio (together with Donald Beekman and Liza Enebeis) and have given type workshops around the world.

When did you decide to work together?
Underware: We met while studying type design and typography at the Royal Academy of Art in The Hague, the Netherlands. We started to work together and decided to call ourselves Underground Typestudio, which sounded to us like an '80s style hobby group trying to be cool, but actually wasn't. It was also our reaction to the really serious type business, and to really serious sounding type foundry names. We didn't want that.

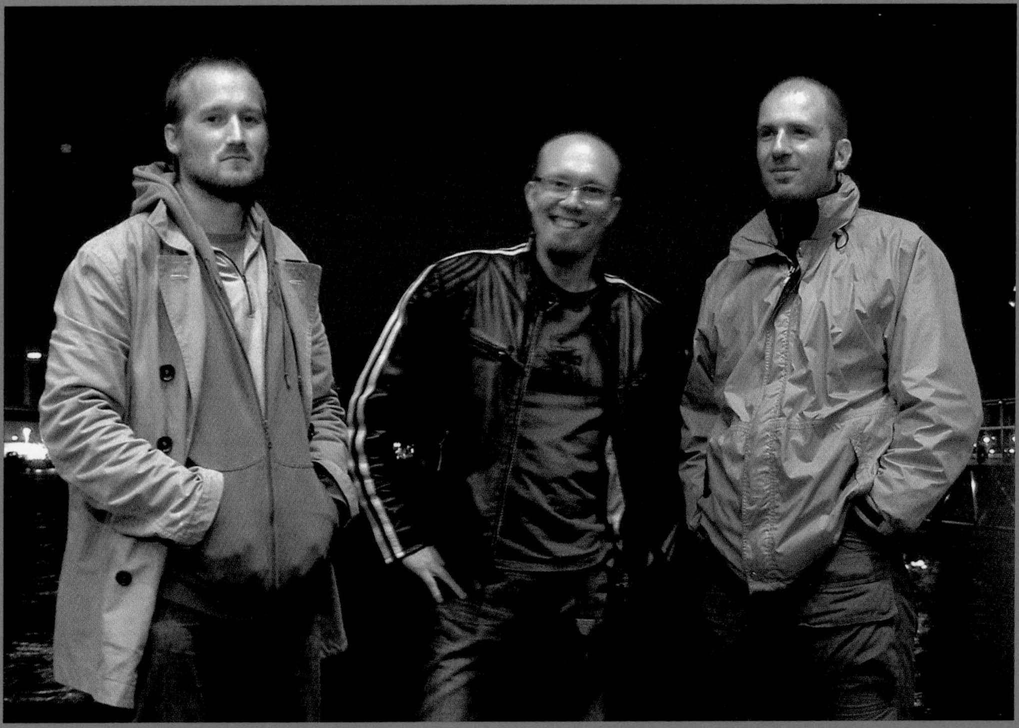

To test our brand we even made Underground Typestudio T-shirts with an early version of Sauna Black Italic. After a while the name stopped sounding convincing to us so we looked for something shorter. Then, our Spanish friend and type designer Joan Carles Casasín stopped off in The Hague – Joan had earlier established a type foundry called Typerware with Andreu Balius. One night, during a party, we decided to make the two groups collide. We needed a name for when we signed an official contract. Mix Underground Typestudio and Typerware together and there you've got it – stuck together for life.

Was type design and lettering something that you had been interested in even before starting your studies at the Academy, or was it something that developed out of other interests?
Underware: There wasn't anything like a key moment – it just developed over time. You go to college, you choose what you want to study – graphic design in our case – and some students are more illustrative, some are more Photoshoppers, and others are more interested in type design and typography. So the three of us opted for the academy in The Hague, with its postgraduate studies in type design and typography.

How does your cooperation work in practice?
Underware: We have a totally merged collaboration. It's impossible to define who does what, as this varies all the time and totally depends on the situation. There are no basic guidelines for our cooperation. One person continues where the other left off, while a third drops in new ideas from the sidelines. Most of the communication goes through e-mail and phone.
We feel it's not that important which one of us is the creator of something. The essence of our collaboration is that none of us would individually arrive at our final destination. It takes three for a synergystic tango. Producing type is still something you can only do in cooperation with others. To make good products you need the help of specialists, as it's impossible to know everything yourself.
For those desperately seeking a description of our working process: sorry, we can't provide such a thing as it doesn't exist. It's probably hard for an outsider to imagine, but for us it's totally logical and natural. We are a unified being.
This might not be a satisfactory answer, as pigeonholing is human nature, but Underware can't be compartmentalised.

Are you primarily inspired by each other or by forces from the outside?
Underware: Both. Inspiration is a complex thing. As I've said, all three of us share the work, so inspiration automatically comes from all kinds of directions. We might get our inspiration from yoga, Karelian pies, riding bikes and waves, watching clouds, Spätzel, culture in its broadest sense, any kind of subculture, jumping in a hole in the ice, German sausages or a relaxed sauna. We also appreciate our daily chocolate, especially Nutella. All this keeps us going. Seeing two very beautiful plants with incredible shapes the other day at the Botanical Garden was something really amazing. Unimaginably beautiful.
When it comes to type design, all of this matters. Call it inspiration. For outsiders, it often seems as though there is only a very little space for creativity in type design, but that's not true. Of course, within such a conventional area as text typefaces, you also need to know about the

Previous page, from left to right: Bas Jacobs, Sami Kortemäki and Akiem Helmling. Opposite, top: sketches for the Auto font family. Bottom: sketches for the typeface Liza.

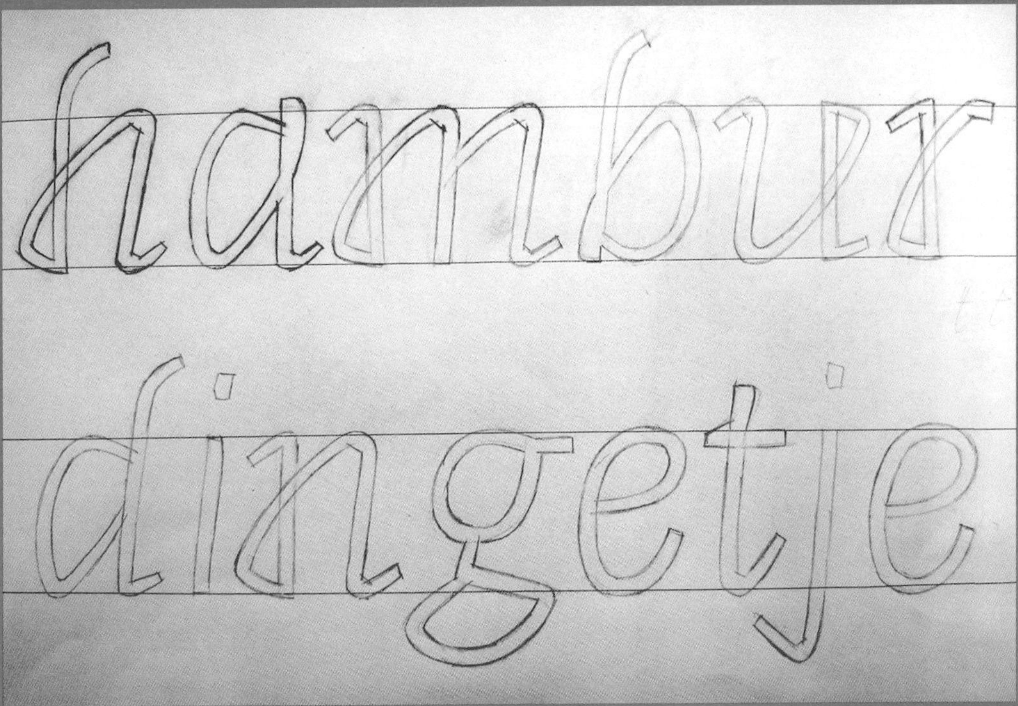
hambur
dingetje

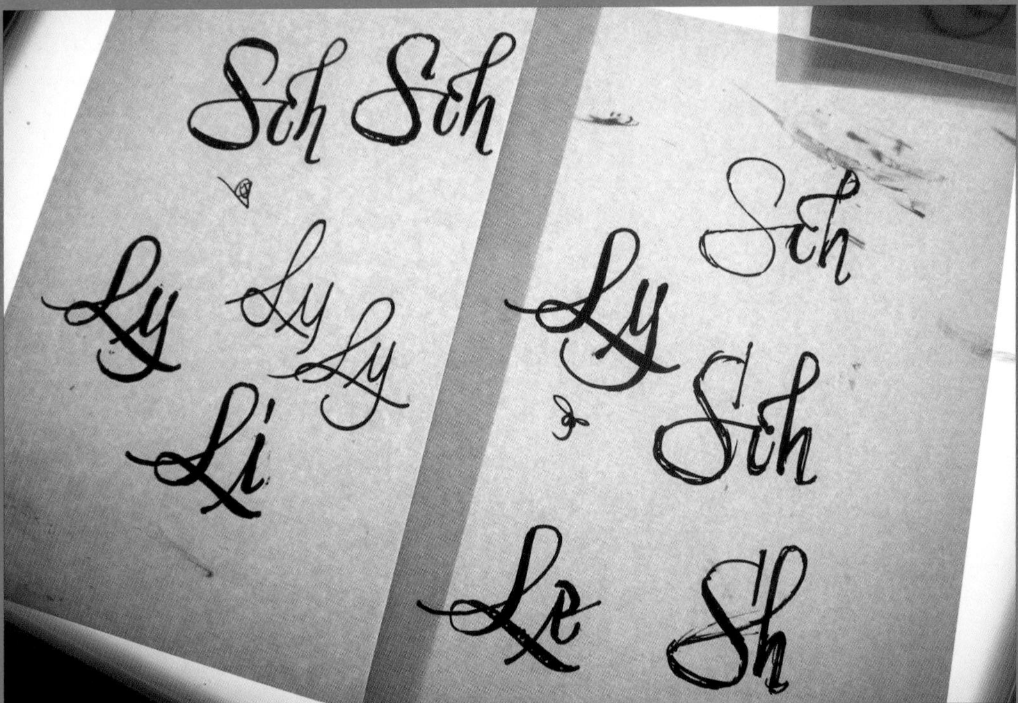
Sch Sch
Ly Ly Ly
Li
Sch
Ly
Sch
Le Sh

history of type design and typography. This kind of knowledge can also be inspiring.

You've given quite a lot of type workshops, brought out publications, started Typeradio and organised the Now We Are Talking Festival. What place do these other activities have within your group and is type design the main focus of its members?
Underware: We feel it's important to place things into a bigger context. So, from the start, drawing type was only one part of our daily activity. Language research, programming, poetry, and stuff like Typeradio and the *Now We Are Talking Festival* are logical consequences of this approach. In the beginning we also did graphic design work, like websites, but that part of our business hardly exists any more.
It's sometimes hard to say what takes up most of our time. It changes constantly. The plot is to not have a plot. Basically we spend our time on what we think makes sense, or seems to be most important to us at the moment.
Because we let ourselves be surprised where our projects take us, things can get a bit out of hand sometimes, but with satisfying results. Like, for example, with the *Now We Are Talking Festival.* In 2010–2011, with Typeradio, we interviewed four type legends: Ed Benguiat, Wim Crouwel, Adrian Frutiger and Gerrit Noordzij. After the interviews were finished, we selected four musicians/composers to write some music, inspired by the interviews. Next, we forwarded the music and interviews to four younger designers, to design the sleeves. Finally, we asked Ellen Lupton to write a short essay, to put the whole project into a wider context. At the end we decided to publish the whole project as a box, including four 7" singles containing the music, four CDs with the interviews and a small booklet. We started looking for a good event where we could present and launch the project, but we weren't able to find anything suitable. So we decided to create our own event, which became the *Now We Are Talking Festival.* While taking what we do seriously, we try not to take ourselves too seriously. As I said before, the goal is to not have a goal. This hasn't changed since we've started.

You've published books to promote several of your fonts, which include a CD containing the full font family, so a designer can test it before buying a commercial licence. Are there enough honest designers out there to support this original way of distributing your fonts?
Underware: All three of us can afford to pay the rent and buy sweeties for the kids. So in that sense you can say yes, it works out. Of course, you don't know how many illegal users there are (compared with legal), and how many licences we would have sold if we hadn't included the CDs with the book. Including the CD feels like offering people the option of test-driving a car before they actually buy it. Logical and necessary at the same time.

Your pixel font Unibody, with its original upright italic, is an original approach to screen fonts. Why did you decide to give it away for free?
Underware: Making a font like Unibody doesn't take much time compared with other fonts. For us, at least, that's why it also wasn't such a problem giving away a font like this for free. At the same time it was also a test, to see what would happen if we gave away a font for free. Would it be used much more than the other fonts that we are selling? Would people appreciate and love it as much as the ones that are for sale? In the end, all these questions are very hard to answer, because you don't know how it would have been if you had made another decision, like giving away another font for free, or selling Unibody.

Alt Type Foundry

alt-foundry.com
contact@alt-foundry.com

Alt Aeon – Black | Andreas Leonidou

THE FOX

ABCDEFGHIJKLMNOPQR
STUVWXYZ0123456789

Alt Aeon – Medium | Andreas Leonidou

THE FOX

ABCDEFGHIJKLMNOPQR
STUVWXYZ0123456789

Alt Geko | Andreas Leonidou

FOX JUMPS OVER

ABCDEFGHIJKLMNOPQRS
TUVWXYZ0123456789

Alt Alternative – Light | Andreas Leonidou

THE FOX JUMPS

ABCDEFGHIJKLMNOPQRSTUVWXYZ0123456789

Alt Alternative – Regular | Andreas Leonidou

JUMPS OVER

ABCDEFGHIJKLMNOPQRSTUVWXYZ0123456789

Alt Alternative – Bold | Andreas Leonidou

FOX JUMPS

ABCDEFGHIJKLMNOPQRSTUVWXYZ0123456789

Alt Fatgami	Andreas Leonidou

JUMPS OVER

ABCDEFGHIJKLMN
OPQRSTUVWXYZ
0123456789

Alt Lautus – Thin	Andreas Leonidou

THE QUICK BROWN FOX JUMPS

ABCDEFGHIJKLMNOPQRSTUVWXYZabcdefghij
klmnopqrstuvwxyz0123456789

Alt Lautus – Thin Italic	Andreas Leonidou

THE QUICK BROWN FOX JUMPS

ABCDEFGHIJKLMNOPQRSTUVWXYZabcdefghij
klmnopqrstuvwxyz0123456789

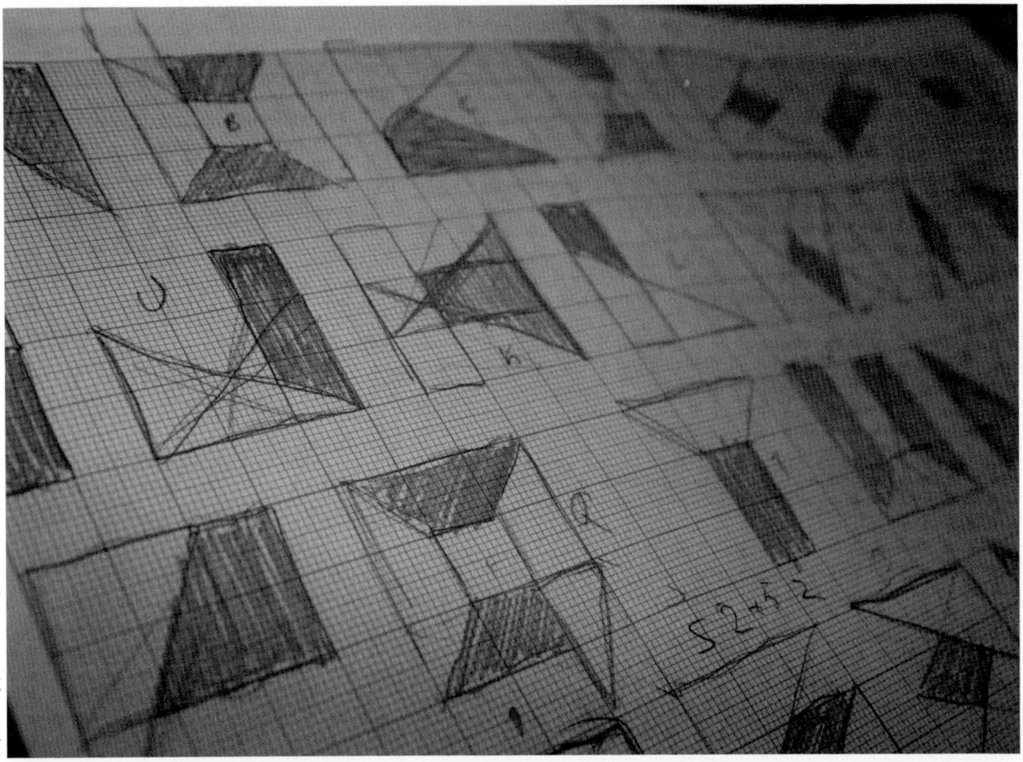

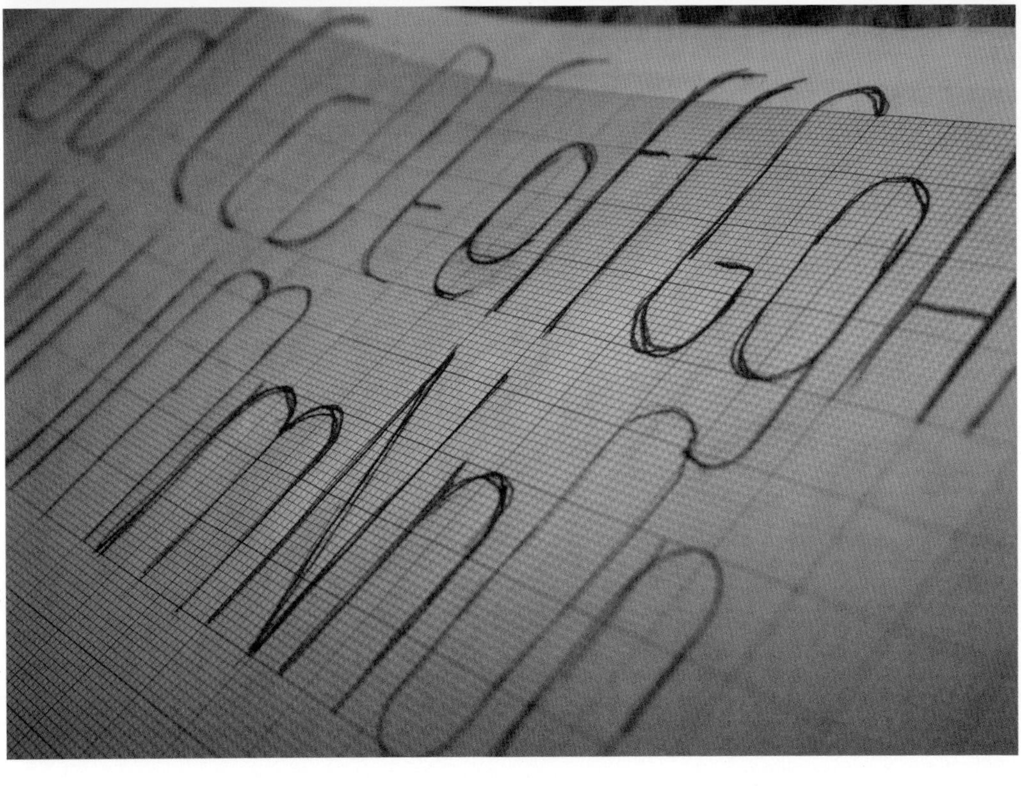

Sketches for the typefaces Fatgami (top) and Lautus (bottom). © 2012 Andreas Leonidou | Alt Type Foundry

Alt Matey v2 – Black | Andreas Leonidou

the quick brown fox jumps

ABCDEFGHIJKLMNOPQRSTUVWXYZabcdefg
hijklmnopqrstuvwxyz0123456789

Alt Mun | Andreas Leonidou

Quick brown fox

ABCDEFGHIJKLMNOPQRSTUVWXYZ
abcdefghijklmnopqrstuvwxyz0123456789&€

Alt Tiwo – Black | Andreas Leonidou

THE FOX

ABCDEFGHIJKLM
NOPQRSTUVWXY
Z0123456789

Alt Tiwo – Light | Andreas Leonidou

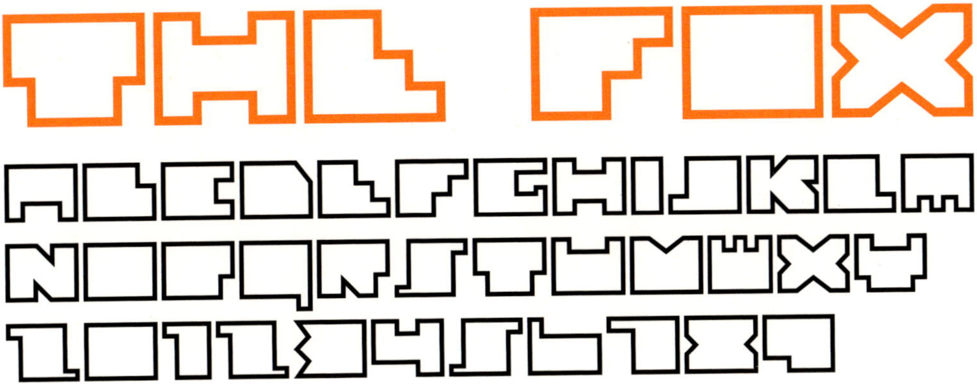

Alt Tiwo – Round | Andreas Leonidou

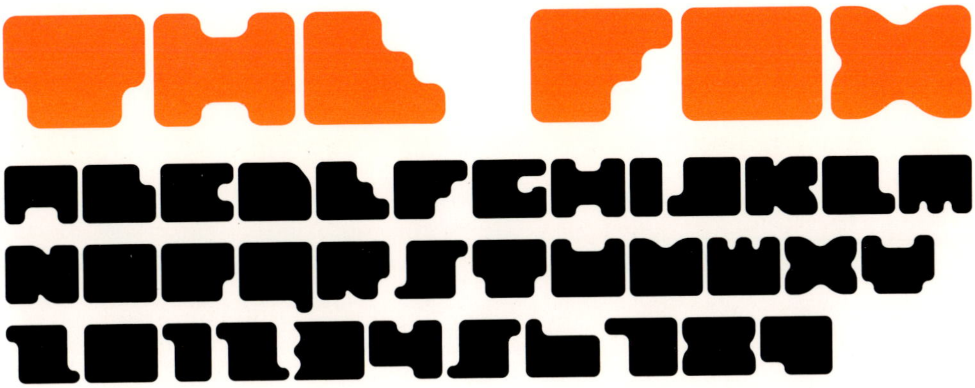

Alt Tiwo – Bend | Andreas Leonidou

Alt Retro – Black | Andreas Leonidou

THE FOX

ABCDEFGHIJKLMNOPQR

STUVWXYZ0123456789

Alt UAV31 | Andreas Leonidou

BROWN FOX

ABCDEFGHIJKL

MNOPQRSTUVW

XYZ0123456789

Alt Vxtll | Andreas Leonidou

QUICK BROWN

ABCDEFGHIJKLMNOPQR

STUVWXYZabcdefghijklmn

opqrstuvwxyz0123456789

Ancymonic

ancymonic.com
info@ancymonic.com

Signika – Light	Anna Giedryś

The quick brown fox jumps

ABCDEFGHIJKLMNOPQRSTUV
WXYZabcdefghijklmnopqrstuv
wxyząçě0123456789(&:;!?$£€)
ABCDEFGHIJKLMNOPQRSTUVWX
YZ0123456789

THE QUICK BROWN FOX jumps over a lazy dog. Zwei Boxkämpfer jagen Eva quer durch Sylt. Lorem ipsum dolor sit amet, consectetur adipisicing elit, sed do eiusmod tempor incididunt ut labore et dolore magna aliqua. The quick brown fox jumps over a lazy dog. Zwei

Signika – Regular	Anna Giedryś

The quick brown fox jumps

ABCDEFGHIJKLMNOPQRSTUV
WXYZabcdefghijklmnopqrstuv
wxyząçě0123456789(&!?$£¥€)
ABCDEFGHIJKLMNOPQRSTUVWX
YZ0123456789

THE QUICK BROWN FOX jumps over a lazy dog. Zwei Boxkämpfer jagen Eva quer durch Sylt. Lorem ipsum dolor sit amet, consectetur adipisicing elit, sed do eiusmod tempor incididunt ut labore et dolore magna aliqua. The quick brown fox jumps over a lazy dog.

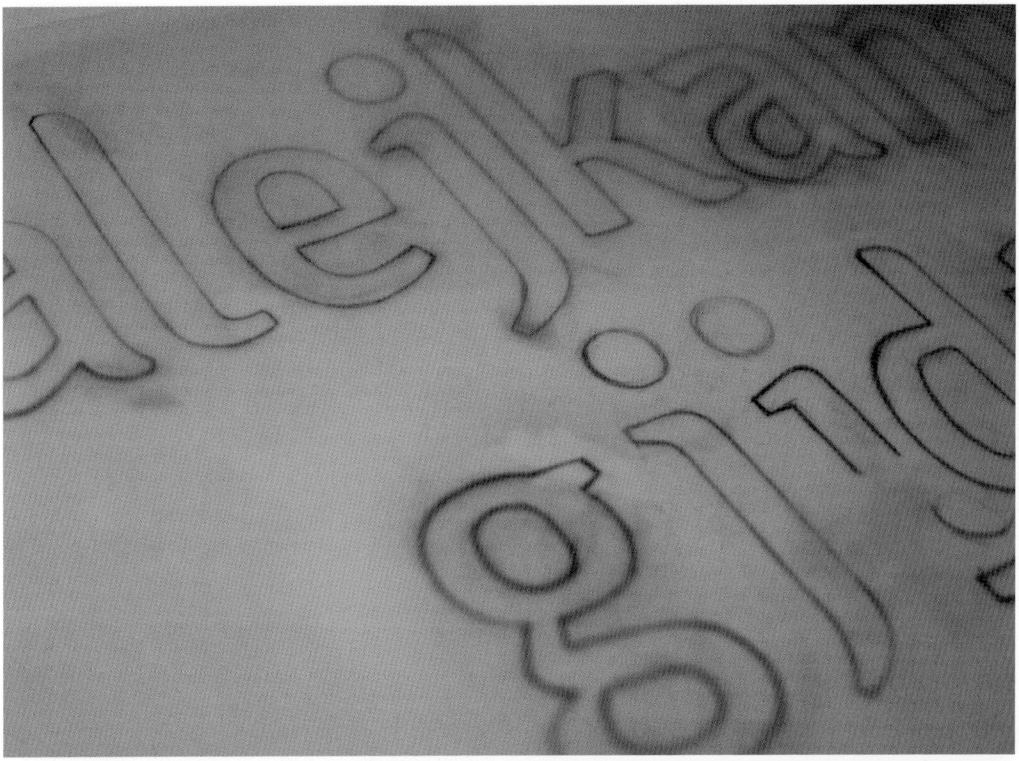

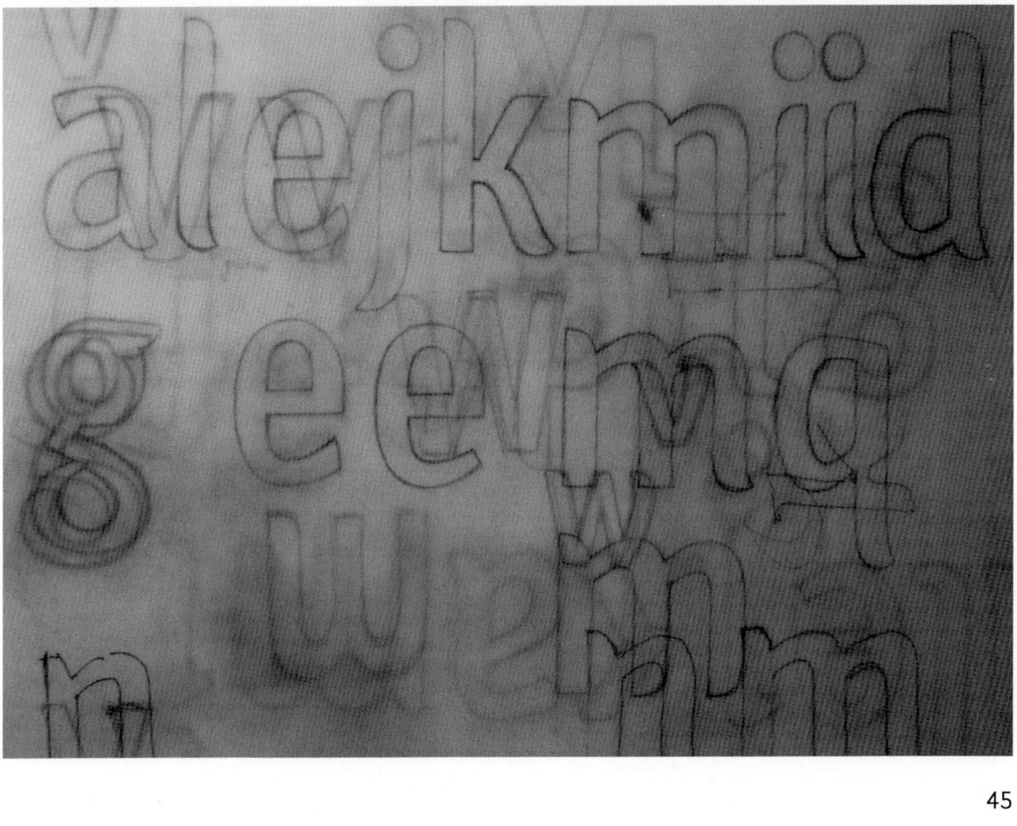

Sketches for the typeface Signika. © 2012 Anna Giedryś | Ancymonic

Signika – Semibold	Anna Giedryś

Brown fox jumps over the

ABCDEFGHIJKLMNOPQRSTUV
WXYZabcdefghijklmnopqrstuv
wxyząçě0123456789(&:;!?$£€)
ABCDEFGHIJKLMNOPQRSTUVW
XYZ0123456789

THE QUICK BROWN FOX jumps over a lazy dog. Zwei Boxkämpfer jagen Eva quer durch Sylt. Lorem ipsum dolor sit amet, consectetur adipisicing elit, sed do eiusmod tempor incididunt ut labore et dolore magna aliqua. The quick brown fox jumps over a lazy dog.

Signika – Bold	Anna Giedryś

Brown fox jumps over the

ABCDEFGHIJKLMNOPQRSTU
VWXYZabcdefghijklmnopqrst
uvwxyząçě012345678(&!?$€)
ABCDEFGHIJKLMNOPQRSTUVW
XYZ0123456789

THE QUICK BROWN FOX jumps over a lazy dog. Zwei Boxkämpfer jagen Eva quer durch Sylt. Lorem ipsum dolor sit amet, consectetur adipisicing elit, sed do eiusmod tempor incididunt ut labore et dolore magna aliqua. The quick brown fox jumps over a lazy dog.

Backpacker

backpacker.gr
contact@backpacker.gr

BP Apeloig | George Triantafyllakos

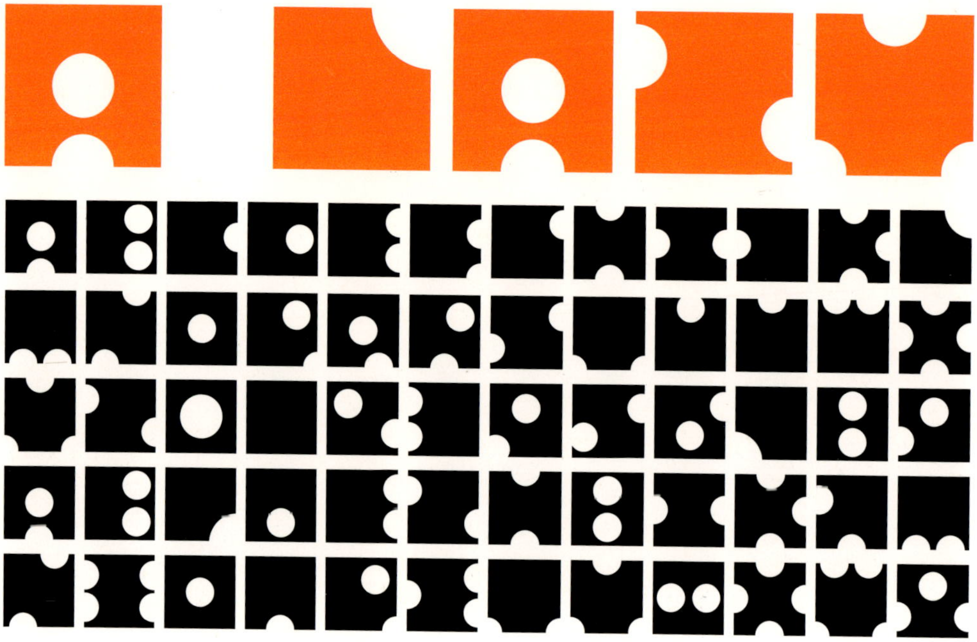

BP Apeloig Open | George Triantafyllakos

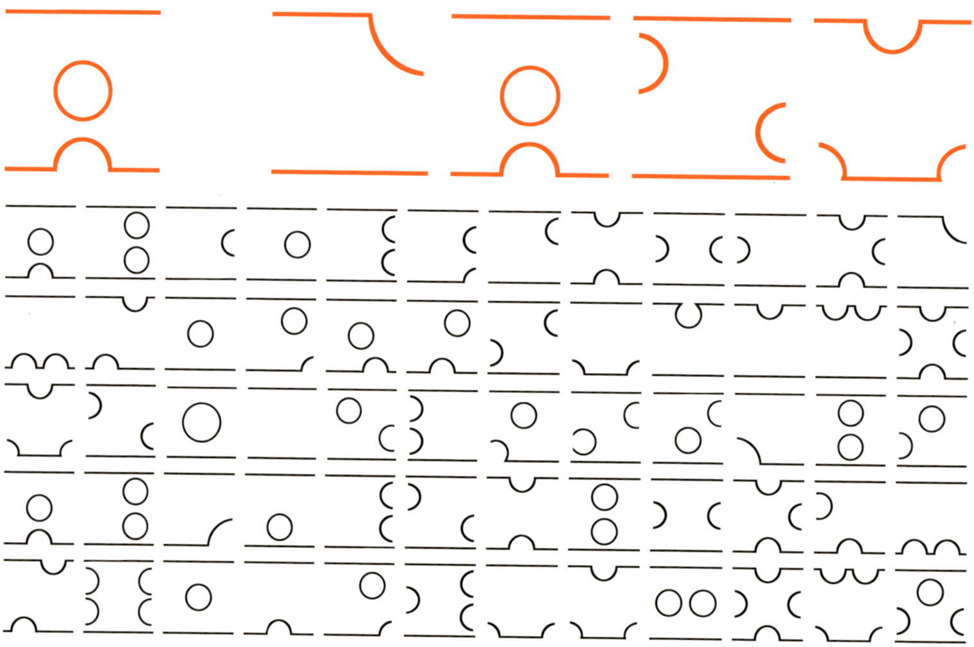

BP Chubby | George Triantafyllakos

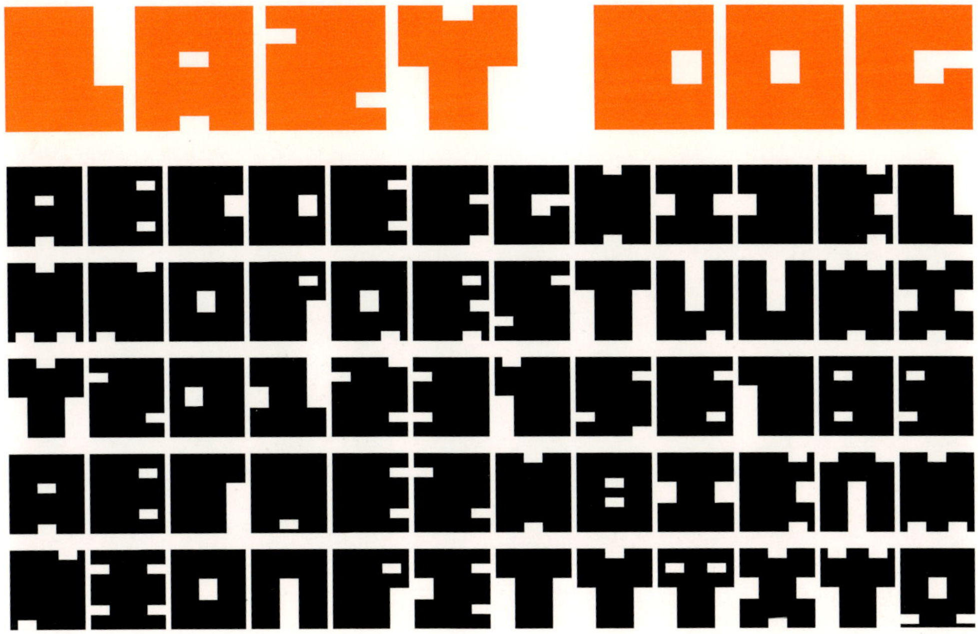

BP Chubby Fat | George Triantafyllakos

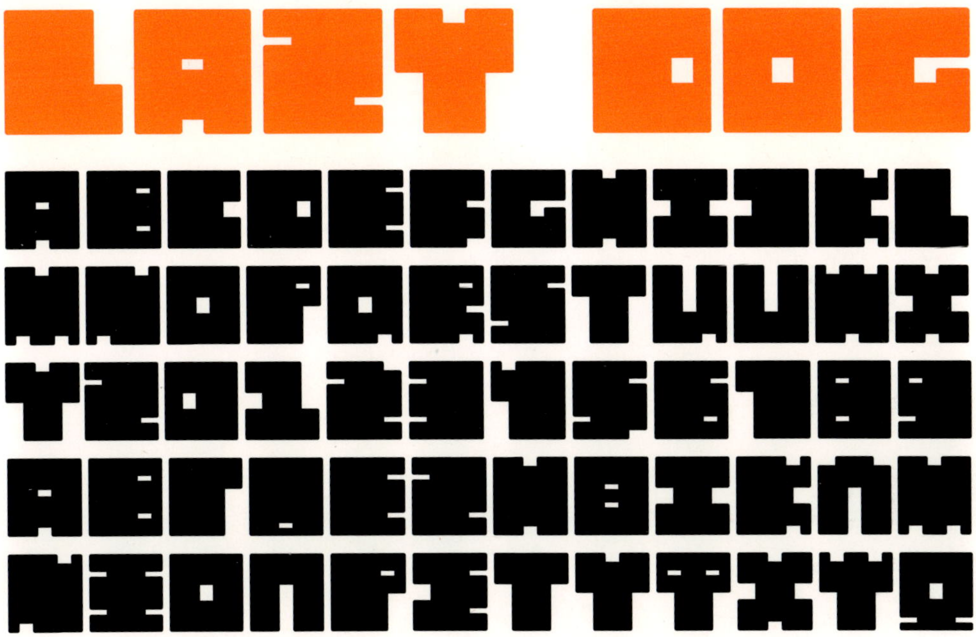

BP Diet – Ultra Black	George Triantafyllakos

brown fox

ABCDEFGHIJKLMNOPQ
RSTUVWXYZabcdefgh
ijklmnopqrstuvwxyz
0123456789(&:;!?$£¥€)
ΑΒΓΔΕΖΗΘΙΚΛΜΝΞΟΠ
ΡΣΤΥΦΧΨΩαβγδεζηθι
κλμνξοπρσςτυφχψω

BP Diet – Ultra Black Italic	George Triantafyllakos

brown fox

ABCDEFGHIJKLMNOPQ
RSTUVWXYZabcdefgh
ijklmnopqrstuvwxyz
0123456789(&:;!?$£¥€)
ΑΒΓΔΕΖΗΘΙΚΛΜΝΞΟΠ
ΡΣΤΥΦΧΨΩαβγδεζηθι
κλμνξοπρσςτυφχψω

Brown fox

Regular

ABCDEFGHIJKLMNOPQRSTUVWXY
Zabcdefghijklmnopqrstuvwx
yząçê0123456789(&!?$£¥€@)
ABCDEFGHIJKLMNOPQRSTUVWXY
Z0123456789
ΑΒΓΔΕΖΗΘΙΚΛΜΝΞΟΠΡΣΤΥΦΧΨΩ
αβγδεζηθικλμνξοπρσςτυφχψω
ΑΒΓΔΕΖΗΘΙΚΛΜΝΞΟΠΡΣΤΥΦΧΨΩ

Light

ABCDEFGHIJKLMNOPQRSTUVWXY
Zabcdefghijklmnopqrstuvwx
yząçê0123456789(&!?$£¥€@)

Bold

ABCDEFGHIJKLMNOPQRSTUVWXY
Zabcdefghijklmnopqrstuvwx
yząçê0123456789(&!?$£¥€@)

BP Dots (cont'd) | George Triantafyllakos

Diamond Light

ABCDEFGHIJKLMNOPQRSTUVWXY
Zabcdefghijklmnopqrstuvwx
yząçě0123456789(&!?$£¥€@)

Diamond Regular

ABCDEFGHIJKLMNOPQRSTUVWXY
Zabcdefghijklmnopqrstuvwx
yząçě0123456789(&!?$£¥€@)

Diamond Bold

ABCDEFGHIJKLMNOPQRSTUVWXY
Zabcdefghijklmnopqrstuvwx
yząçě0123456789(&!?$£¥€@)

Minus Regular

ABCDEFGHIJKLMNOPQRSTUVWXY
Zabcdefghijklmnopqrstuvwx
yząçě0123456789(&!?$£¥€@)

Minus Bold

ABCDEFGHIJKLMNOPQRSTUVWXY
Zabcdefghijklmnopqrstuvwx
yząçě0123456789(&!?$£¥€@)

Plus Regular

ABCDEFGHIJKLMNOPQRSTUVWXY
Zabcdefghijklmnopqrstuvwx
yząçĕ0123456789(&!?$£¥€@)

Plus Bold

ABCDEFGHIJKLMNOPQRSTUVWXY
Zabcdefghijklmnopqrstuvwx
yząçĕ0123456789(&!?$£¥€@)

Squares Light

ABCDEFGHIJKLMNOPQRSTUVWXY
Zabcdefghijklmnopqrstuvwx
yząçĕ0123456789(&!?$£¥€@)

Squares Regular

ABCDEFGHIJKLMNOPQRSTUVWXY
Zabcdefghijklmnopqrstuvwx
yząçĕ0123456789(&!?$£¥€@)

Squares Bold

ABCDEFGHIJKLMNOPQRSTUVWXY
Zabcdefghijklmnopqrstuvwx
yząçĕ0123456789(&!?$£¥€@)

Vertical Regular

ABCDEFGHIJKLMNOPQRSTUVWXY
Zabcdefghijklmnopqrstuvwx
yząçě0123456789(&!?$£¥€@)

Vertical Bold

ABCDEFGHIJKLMNOPQRSTUVWXY
Zabcdefghijklmnopqrstuvwx
yząçě0123456789(&!?$£¥€@)

Condensed

The quick brown fox jumps over a lazy
ABCDEFGHIJKLMNOPQRSTUVWXYZabcdefg
hijklmnopqrstuvwxyząçě0123456789&

Condensed Diamond

ABCDEFGHIJKLMNOPQRSTUVWXYZabcdefg
hijklmnopqrstuvwxyząçě0123456789&

Condensed Square

ABCDEFGHIJKLMNOPQRSTUVWXYZabcdefg
hijklmnopqrstuvwxyząçě0123456789&

Unicase Light

ABCDEFGHIJKLMNOPQRSTUV
WXYZabcdefghijklmnopqr
stuvwxyząçě0123456789$

Unicase Regular

ABCDEFGHIJKLMNOPQRSTUV
WXYZabcdefghijklmnopqr
stuvwxyząçě0123456789$

Unicase Bold

ABCDEFGHIJKLMNOPQRSTUV
WXYZabcdefghijklmnopqr
stuvwxyząçě0123456789$

Unicase Diamond Light

ABCDEFGHIJKLMNOPQRSTUV
WXYZabcdefghijklmnopqr
stuvwxyząçě0123456789$

Unicase Diamond Regular

ABCDEFGHIJKLMNOPQRSTUV
WXYZabcdefghijklmnopqr
stuvwxyząçě0123456789$

Unicase Diamond Bold

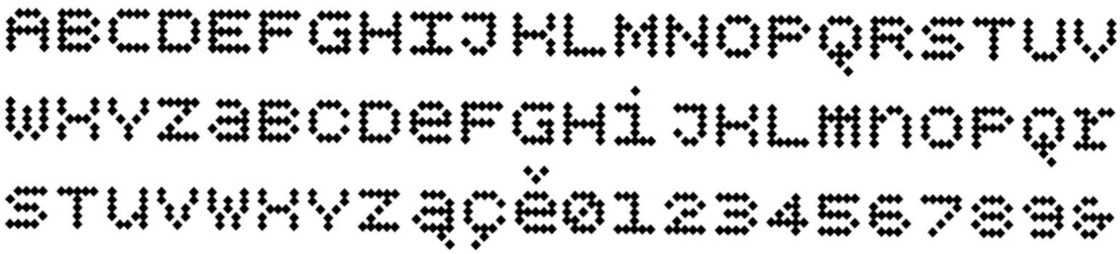

Unicase Minus Regular

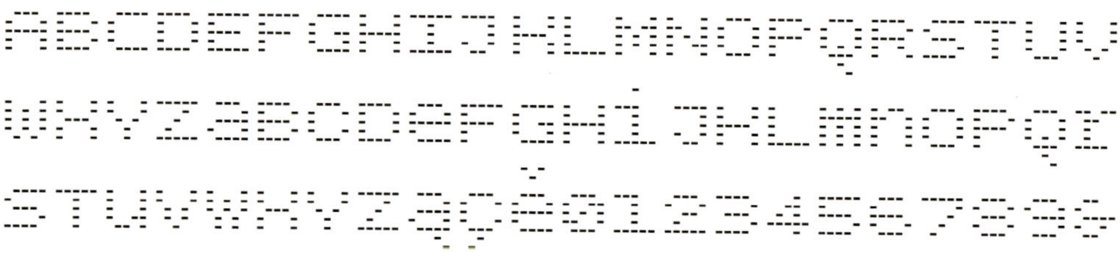

Unicase Minus Bold

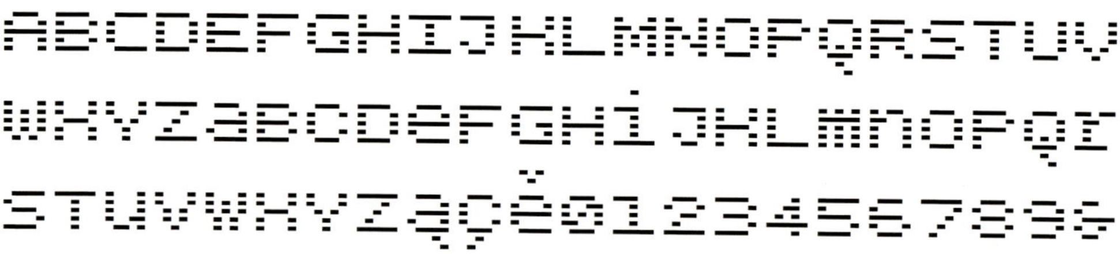

Unicase Plus Regular

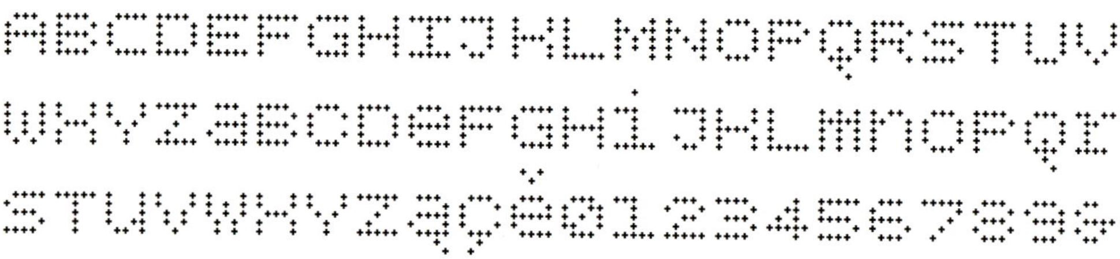

Unicase Plus Bold

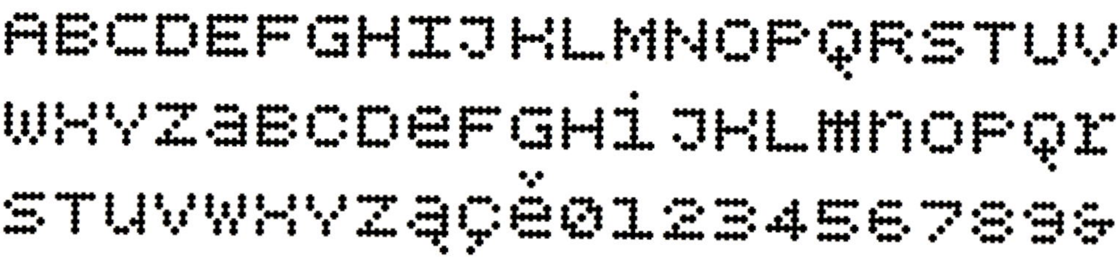

Unicase Square Light

ABCDEFGHIJKLMNOPQRSTUV
WXYZabcdefghijklmnopqr
stuvwxyząçě0123456789$

Unicase Square Regular

ABCDEFGHIJKLMNOPQRSTUV
WXYZabcdefghijklmnopqr
stuvwxyząçě0123456789$

Unicase Square Bold

ABCDEFGHIJKLMNOPQRSTUV
WXYZabcdefghijklmnopqr
stuvwxyząçě0123456789$

Unicase Vertical Regular

ABCDEFGHIJKLMNOPQRSTUVWXY
Zabcdefghijklmnopqrstuvwx
yząçě0123456789(&!?$£¥€@)

Unicase Vertical Bold

ABCDEFGHIJKLMNOPQRSTUV
WXYZabcdefghijklmnopqr
stuvwxyząçě0123456789$

BP Mono – Regular	George Triantafyllakos

Quick brown

ABCDEFGHIJKLMNOPQRSTUVWXYZ
abcdefghijklmnopqrstuvwxyz
0123456789(&:;!?$£¥€)
ΑΒΓΔΕΖΗΘΙΚΛΜΝΞΟΠΡΣΤΥΦΧΨΩαβ
γδεζηθικλμνξοπρσςτυφχψω

THE QUICK BROWN FOX jumps over a lazy dog. Lorem ipsum dolor sit amet, consectetur adipisicing elit, sed do eiusmod tempor incididunt ut labore et dolore magna aliqua. The quick brown fox

BP Mono – Italic	George Triantafyllakos

Quick brown

ABCDEFGHIJKLMNOPQRSTUVWXYZ
abcdefghijklmnopqrstuvwxyz
0123456789(&:;!?$£¥€)
ΑΒΓΔΕΖΗΘΙΚΛΜΝΞΟΠΡΣΤΥΦΧΨΩαβ
γδεζηθικλμνξοπρσςτυφχψω

THE QUICK BROWN FOX jumps over a lazy dog. Lorem ipsum dolor sit amet, consectetur adipisicing elit, sed do eiusmod tempor incididunt ut labore et dolore magna aliqua. The quick brown fox

BP Mono – Bold	George Triantafyllakos

Quick brown

ABCDEFGHIJKLMNOPQRSTUVWXYZ
abcdefghijklmnopqrstuvwxyz
0123456789(&:;!?$£¥€)
ΑΒΓΔΕΖΗΘΙΚΛΜΝΞΟΠΡΣΤΥΦΧΨΩαβ
γδεζηθικλμνξοπρσςτυφχψω

THE QUICK BROWN FOX jumps over a lazy dog. Lorem ipsum dolor sit amet, consectetur adipisicing elit, sed do eiusmod tempor incididunt ut labore et dolore magna aliqua. The quick brown fox

BP Mono – Stencil Bold	George Triantafyllakos

The quick brown FOX JUMPS

ABCDEFGHIJKLMNOPQRSTUVWXYZ
abcdefghijklmnopqrstuvwxyz
0123456789(&:;!?$£¥€)
ΑΒΓΔΕΖΗΘΙΚΛΜΝΞΟΠΡΣΤΥΦΧΨΩαβ
γδεζηθικλμνξοπρσςτυφχψω

BP Imperial | George Triantafyllakos

BROWN FOX JUMPS OVER

Light

ABCDEFGHIJKLMNOPQRSTUVWXYZ

0123456789(&.,:;!?$€@)

ΑΒΓΔΕΖΗΘΙΚΛΜΝΞΟΠΡΣΤΥΦΧΨΩ

Light Italic

ABCDEFGHIJKLMNOPQRSTUVWXYZ

0123456789(&.,:;!?$€@)

Regular

ABCDEFGHIJKLMNOPQRSTUVWXYZ

0123456789(&.,:;!?$€@)

Italic

ABCDEFGHIJKLMNOPQRSTUVWXYZ

0123456789(&.,:;!?$€@)

Brown fox LAZY DOG

Regular

A B C D E F G H I J K L M N O P Q R S T U V W X Y
Z a b c d e f g h i j k l m n o p q r s t u v w x
y z 0 1 2 3 4 5 6 7 8 9 (& : ; ! ? $ £ ¥ € @)
Α Β Γ Δ Ε Ζ Η Θ Ι Κ Λ Μ Ν Ξ Ο Π Ρ Σ Τ Υ Φ Χ Ψ Ω α
β γ δ ε ζ η θ ι κ λ μ ν ξ ο π ρ σ ς τ υ φ χ ψ ω

Italic

A B C D E F G H I J K L M N O P Q R S T U V W X Y
Z a b c d e f g h i j k l m n o p q r s t u v w x
y z 0 1 2 3 4 5 6 7 8 9 (& : ; ! ? $ £ ¥ € @)

Slashed

A B C D E F G H I J K L M N O P Q R S T U V W X Y
Z a b c d e f g h i j k l m n o p q r s t u v w x
y z 0 1 2 3 4 5 6 7 8 9 (& : ; ! ? $ £ ¥ € @)

Backpacker | backpacker.gr

Slashed Italic

ABCDEFGHIJKLMNOPQRSTUVWXY
Zabcdefghijklmnopqrstuvwx
yz0123456789(&:;!?$£¥€@)

Strikethrough

~~ABCDEFGHIJKLMNOPQRSTUVWXY~~
~~Zabcdefghijklmnopqrstuvwx~~
~~yz0123456789(&:;!?$£¥€@)~~

Strikethrough Italic

~~*ABCDEFGHIJKLMNOPQRSTUVWXY*~~
~~*Zabcdefghijklmnopqrstuvwx*~~
~~*yz0123456789(&:;!?$£¥€@)*~~

Underscored

ABCDEFGHIJKLMNOPQRSTUVWXY
Zabcdefghijklmnopqrstuvwx
yz0123456789(&:;!?$£¥€@)

Underscored Italic

ABCDEFGHIJKLMNOPQRSTUVWXY
Zabcdefghijklmnopqrstuvwx
yz0123456789(&:;!?$£¥€@)

The quick
brown
fox jumps over
A LAZY DOG
Lorem ipsum
dolor

BP Typewrite Damaged | George Triantafyllakos

Brown fox LAZY DOG

Regular

ABCDEFGHIJKLMNOPQRSTUVWXY
Zabcdefghijklmnopqrstuvwx
yz0123456789(&:;!?$£¥€@)
ΑΒΓΔΕΖΗΘΙΚΛΜΝΞΟΠΡΣΤΥΦΧΨΩα
βγδεζηθικλμνξοπρσςτυφχψω

Italic

ABCDEFGHIJKLMNOPQRSTUVWXY
Zabcdefghijklmnopqrstuvwx
yz0123456789(&:;!?$£¥€@)

Slashed

ABCDEFGHIJKLMNOPQRSTUVWXY
Zabcdefghijklmnopqrstuvwx
yz0123456789(&:;!?$£¥€@)

Slashed Italic

ABCDEFGHIJKLMNOPQRSTUVWXY
Zabcdefghijklmnopqrstuvwx
yz0123456789(&:;!?$£¥€@)

Strikethrough

ABCDEFGHIJKLMNOPQRSTUVWXY
Zabcdefghijklmnopqrstuvwx
yz0123456789(&:;!?$£¥€@)

Strikethrough Italic

ABCDEFGHIJKLMNOPQRSTUVWXY
Zabcdefghijklmnopqrstuvwx
yz0123456789(&:;!?$£¥€@)

Underscored

ABCDEFGHIJKLMNOPQRSTUVWXY
Zabcdefghijklmnopqrstuvwx
yz0123456789(&:;!?$£¥€@)

Underscored Italic

ABCDEFGHIJKLMNOPQRSTUVWXY
Zabcdefghijklmnopqrstuvwx
yz0123456789(&:;!?$£¥€@)

BP Script	George Triantafyllakos

The quick brown fox
jumps over

ABCDEFGHIJKLMNOPQRSTUVW
XYZabcdefghijklmnopqrstuvwxyz
0123456789(&:;¡!?$£¥€@)
ΑΒΓΔΕΖΗΘΙΚΛΜΝΞΟΠΡΣΤΥΦΧΨ
Ωαβγδεζηθικλμνξοπρσςτυφχψω

DPSD Beyond	George Triantafyllakos

The quick brown
fox jumps over

ABCDEFGHIJKLMNOPQRSTUVWXY
Zabcdefghijklmnopqrstuvwx
yz0123456789(&:;!?$£¥€@)
ΑΒΓΔΕΖΗΘΙΚΛΜΝΞΘΠΡΣΤΥΦΧΨΩα
βγδεζηθικλμνξοπρσςτυφχψω

La Boîte Graphique

laboitegraphique.fr
ewen@laboitegraphique.fr

Fanfarone – Regular	Ewen Prigent

JUMPS OVER A

ABCDEFGHIJKLMNOPQRSTU
VWXYZÄÇÉ0123456789(&:;!?€)

Fanfarone – Italique	Ewen Prigent

JUMPS OVER A

ABCDEFGHIJKLMNOPQRSTU
VWXYZÄÇÉ0123456789(&:;!?€)

Fanfarone – Bold	Ewen Prigent

JUMPS OVER A

ABCDEFGHIJKLMNOPQRSTU
VWXYZÄÇÉ0123456789(&:;!?€)

Bunker | Ewen Prigent

THE FOX

ABCDEFGHIJKLMNOPQR
STUVWXYZ0123456789

Gram | Ewen Prigent

BROWN JUMPS

ABCDEFGHIJKLMNOPQRSTUV
WXYZÄÇÉ0123456789[&:;!?]

Ibiscus | Ewen Prigent

THE QUICK BROWN FOX
OVER A LAZY DOG

ABCDEFGHIJKLMNOPQRS
TUVWXYZ0123456789[!?]

Quinto	Ewen Prigent

The brown fox

ABCDEFGHIJKLMNOPQRSTUVW
XYZabcdefghijklmnopqrstuv
wxyzäçé0123456789(&:;!?$£€)

Rondi	Ewen Prigent

the brown fox

abcdefghijklmnopqrstu
vwxyzäçé0123456789&!?€

Rosa	Ewen Prigent

The quick brown fox

ABCDEFGHIJKLMNOPQRSTUVWXY
Zabcdefghijklmnopqrstuvwxy
zäçé0123456789[&:;!?$¢£¥€@]

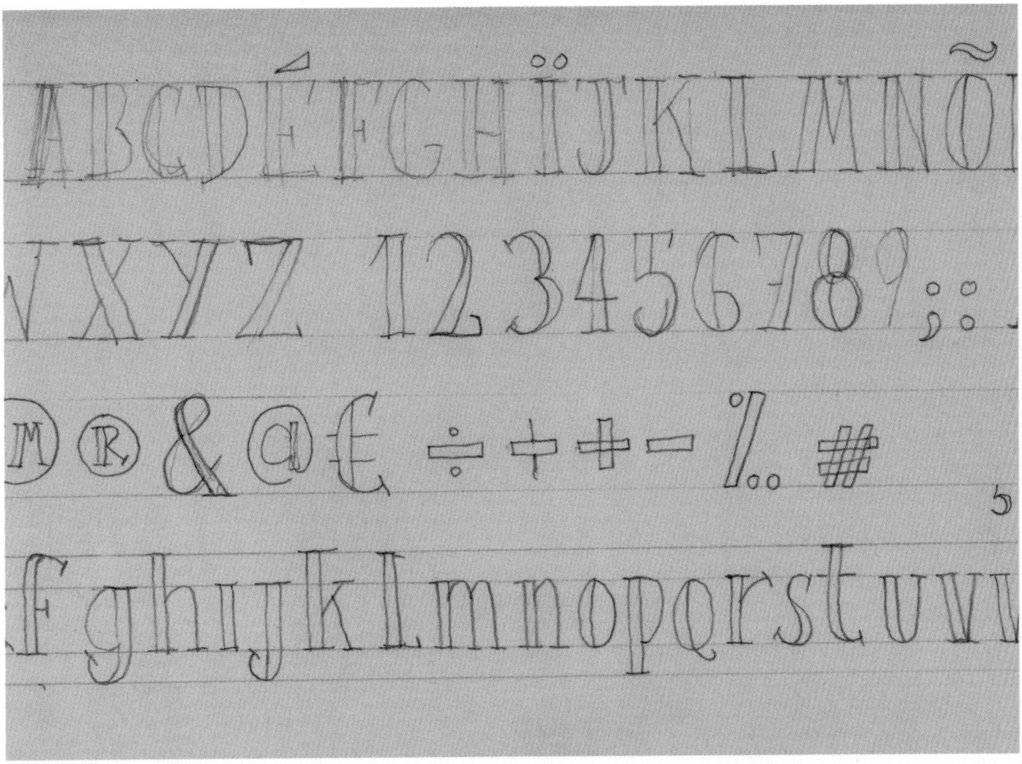

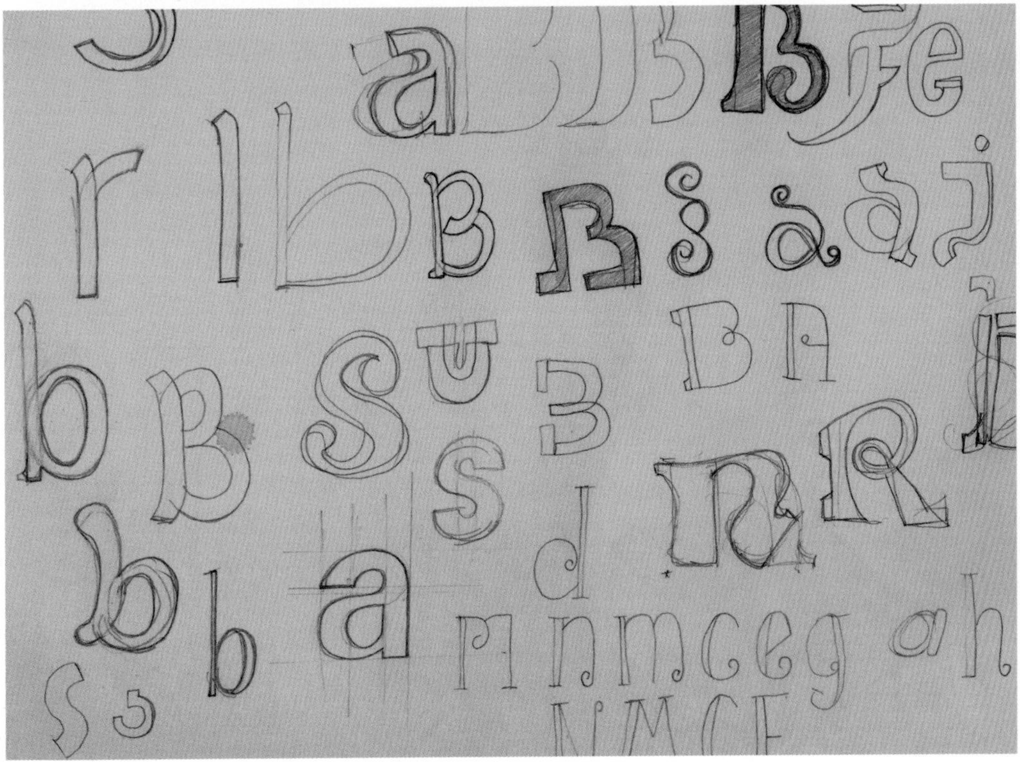

Top: sketches for the typeface Quinto. Bottom: detail from sketchbook page. © 2012 Ewen Prigent | La Boîte Graphique

Trouble – Regular	Ewen Prigent

A LAZY DOG

ABCDEFGHIJKLMNOPQRSTUVWX

YZÄÇÉ0123456789(&:;!?$¢€@)

Trouble – Italique	Ewen Prigent

A LAZY DOG

ABCDEFGHIJKLMNOPQRSTUVWX

YZÄÇÉ0123456789(&:;!?$¢€@)

Trouble – Close Bold	Ewen Prigent

A LAZY DOG

ABCDEFGHIJKLMNOPQRSTUVWX

YZÄÇÉ0123456789(&:;!?$¢€@)

Carrois Type Design

carrois.com
post@carrois.com

Colaborate – Thin | Ralph du Carrois

ABCDEFGHIJKLMNOPQRSTUV
WXYZabcdefghijklmnopqrstuvwx
yzäçé0123456789(&:;!?$¢£¥€@)

THE QUICK BROWN FOX jumps over a lazy dog. Zwei Boxkämpfer jagen Eva quer durch Sylt. Lorem ipsum dolor sit amet, consectetur adipisicing elit, sed do eiusmod tempor incididunt ut labore et dolore magna aliqua. The quick brown fox jumps over a lazy dog. Zwei Boxkämpfer Jagen Eva

Colaborate – Light | Ralph du Carrois

ABCDEFGHIJKLMNOPQRSTU
VWXYZabcdefghijklmnopqrstuv
wxyzäçé0123456789(&:;!?$£¥€)

THE QUICK BROWN FOX jumps over a lazy dog. Zwei Boxkämpfer jagen Eva quer durch Sylt. Lorem ipsum dolor sit amet, consectetur adipisicing elit, sed do eiusmod tempor incididunt ut labore et dolore magna aliqua. The quick brown fox jumps over a lazy dog. Zwei Boxkämpfer

Colaborate – Regular | Ralph du Carrois

ABCDEFGHIJKLMNOPQRSTU
VWXYZabcdefghijklmnopqrst
uvwxyzäçé0123456789(&:;!?€)

THE QUICK BROWN FOX jumps over a lazy dog. Zwei Boxkämpfer jagen Eva quer durch Sylt. Lorem ipsum dolor sit amet, consectetur adipisicing elit, sed do eiusmod tempor incididunt ut labore et dolore magna aliqua. The quick brown fox jumps over a lazy dog. Zwei

The quick
brown
fox jumps over
a lazy dog
ZWEI
Boxkämpfer jagen

Carrois Type Design | carrois.com

Colaborate – Medium	Ralph du Carrois

ABCDEFGHIJKLMNOPQRST
UVWXYZabcdefghijklmnopq
rstuvwxyzäçé0123456789&€

THE QUICK BROWN FOX jumps over a lazy dog. Zwei Boxkämpfer jagen Eva quer durch Sylt. Lorem ipsum dolor sit amet, consectetur adipisicing elit, sed do eiusmod tempor incididunt ut labore et dolore magna aliqua. The quick brown fox jumps over a

Colaborate – Bold	Ralph du Carrois

ABCDEFGHIJKLMNOPQRS
TUVWXYZabcdefghijklmnop
qrstuvwxyzäçé0123456789

THE QUICK BROWN FOX jumps over a lazy dog. Zwei Boxkämpfer jagen Eva quer durch Sylt. Lorem ipsum dolor sit amet, consectetur adipisicing elit, sed do eiusmod tempor incididunt ut labore et dolore magna aliqua. The quick brown fox jumps over

Share – Regular	Ralph du Carrois

ABCDEFGHIJKLMNOPQRSTUVWXY
Zabcdefghijklmnopqrstuvwxyzä
çé0123456789(&:;!?$¢£¥€@)

THE QUICK BROWN FOX jumps over a lazy dog. Zwei Boxkämpfer jagen Eva quer durch Sylt. Lorem ipsum dolor sit amet, consectetur adipisicing elit, sed do eiusmod tempor incididunt ut labore et dolore magna aliqua. The quick brown fox jumps over a lazy dog. Zwei Boxkämpfer

Share – Italic	Ralph du Carrois

ABCDEFGHIJKLMNOPQRSTUVWXY Zabcdefghijklmnopqrstuvwxyzä çé0123456789(&:;!?$¢£¥€@)

THE QUICK BROWN FOX jumps over a lazy dog. Zwei Boxkämpfer jagen Eva quer durch Sylt. Lorem ipsum dolor sit amet, consectetur adipisicing elit, sed do eiusmod tempor incididunt ut labore et dolore magna aliqua. The quick brown fox jumps over a lazy dog. Zwei Boxkämpfer

Share – Bold	Ralph du Carrois

ABCDEFGHIJKLMNOPQRSTUVWX YZabcdefghijklmnopqrstuvwx yzäçé0123456789(&:;!?$¢£¥€@)

THE QUICK BROWN FOX jumps over a lazy dog. Zwei Boxkämpfer jagen Eva quer durch Sylt. Lorem ipsum dolor sit amet, consectetur adipisicing elit, sed do eiusmod tempor incidid-unt ut labore et dolore magna aliqua. The quick brown fox jumps over a lazy dog. Zwei

Share – Bold Italic	Ralph du Carrois

ABCDEFGHIJKLMNOPQRSTUVWX YZabcdefghijklmnopqrstuvwx yzäçé0123456789(&:;!?$¢£¥€@)

THE QUICK BROWN FOX jumps over a lazy dog. Zwei Boxkämpfer jagen Eva quer durch Sylt. Lorem ipsum dolor sit amet, consectetur adipisicing elit, sed do eiusmod tempor incidid-unt ut labore et dolore magna aliqua. The quick brown fox jumps over a lazy dog. Zwei

Share – Tech	Ralph du Carrois

ABCDEFGHIJKLMNOPQRSTUVWXY
Zabcdefghijklmnopqrstuvwxyzä
çé0123456789(&:;!?$¢£¥€@)

THE QUICK BROWN FOX jumps over a lazy dog. Zwei Boxkämpfer jagen Eva quer durch Sylt. Lorem ipsum dolor sit amet, consectetur adipisicing elit, sed do eiusmod tempor incididunt ut labore et dolore magna aliqua. The quick brown fox jumps over a lazy dog. Zwei Boxkämpfer jagen Eva

Share – Tech Mono	Ralph du Carrois

ABCDEFGHIJKLMNOPQRSTUVW
XYZabcdefghijklmnopqrst
uvwxyzäçé0123456789&!?€

THE QUICK BROWN FOX jumps over a lazy dog. Zwei Boxkämpfer jagen Eva quer durch Sylt. Lorem ipsum dolor sit amet, consectetur adipisicing elit, sed do eiusmod tempor incididunt ut labore et dolore magna ali-

Chank Co

chank.com
fonts@chank.com

CoCo Flowerfont – Shadows, Midtones & Highlights | Chank Diesel & Co

QUICK BROWN
JUMPS

ABbCDEFGHIJJKLMMN
OPPQQRSTUUVWWXY
YZZÄÇÉ0123456789¢?

Panefresco – 1wt | Chank Diesel & Co (derived from Titillium)

ABCDEFGHIJKLMNOPQRSTUV
WXYZabcdefghijklmnopqrstu
vwxyząçě0123456789(&!?$€)

THE QUICK BROWN FOX jumps over a lazy dog. Zwei Boxkämpfer jagen Eva quer durch Sylt. Lorem ipsum dolor sit amet, consectetur adipisicing elit, sed do eiusmod tempor incididunt ut labore et dolore magna aliqua. The quick brown fox jumps over a lazy dog.

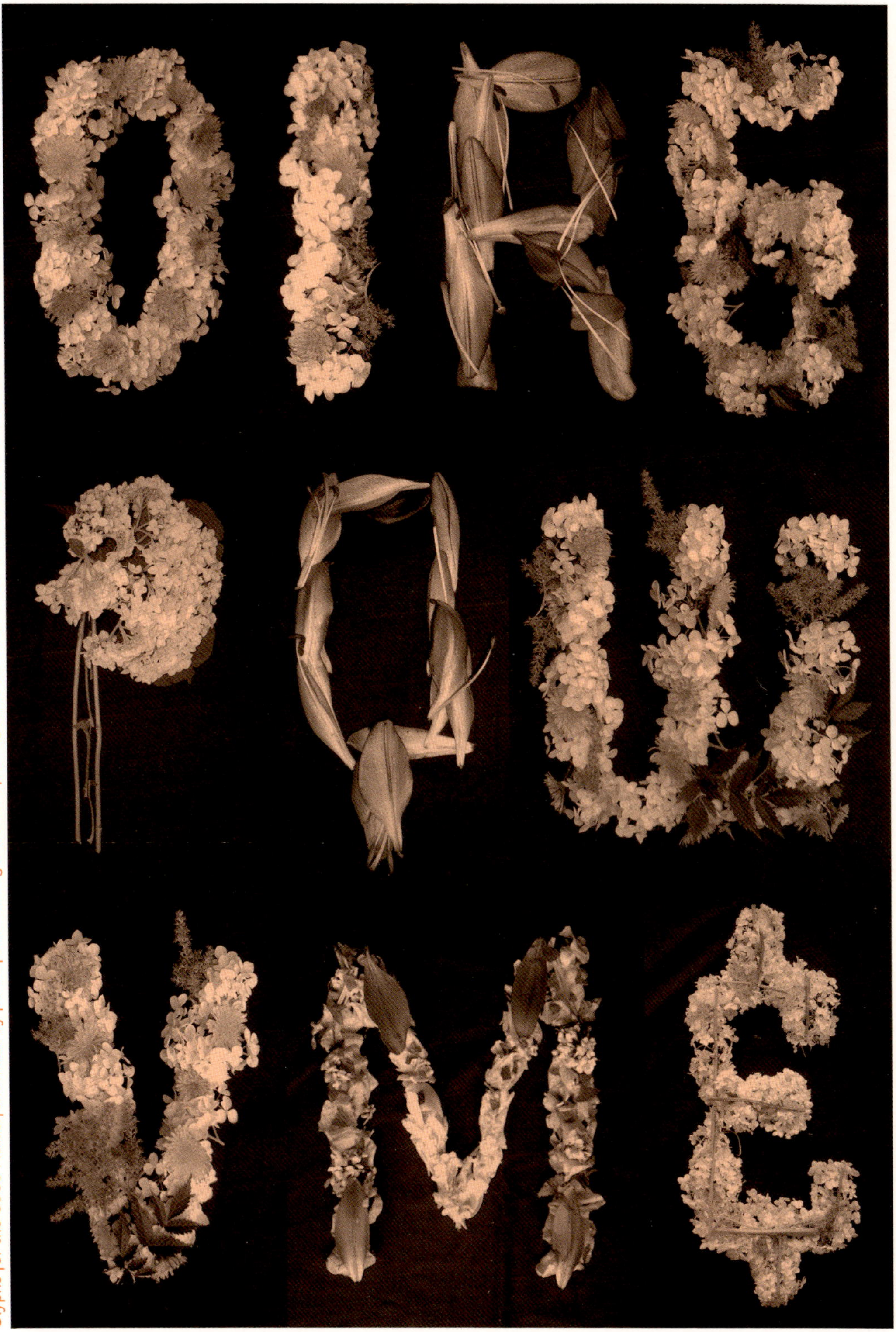

Glyphs for the CoCo Flowerfont made by participants during a workshop on 19 June 2010, at CoCo in Minneapolis. © 2012 Chank Diesel | Chank Co

Panefresco – 1wt Italic	Chank Diesel & Co (derived from Titillium)

ABCDEFGHIJKLMNOPQRSTUV WXYZabcdefghijklmnopqrstu vwxyząçě0123456789(&!?$€)

THE QUICK BROWN FOX jumps over a lazy dog. Zwei Boxkämpfer jagen Eva quer durch Sylt. Lorem ipsum dolor sit amet, consectetur adipisicing elit, sed do eiusmod tempor incididunt ut labore et dolore magna aliqua. The quick brown fox jumps over a lazy dog.

Panefresco – 250wt	Chank Diesel & Co (derived from Titillium)

ABCDEFGHIJKLMNOPQRSTUV WXYZabcdefghijklmnopqrstu vwxyząçě0123456789(&!?$€)

THE QUICK BROWN FOX jumps over a lazy dog. Zwei Boxkämpfer jagen Eva quer durch Sylt. Lorem ipsum dolor sit amet, consectetur adipisicing elit, sed do eiusmod tempor incididunt ut labore et dolore magna aliqua. The quick brown fox jumps over a lazy dog.

Panefresco – 250wt Italic	Chank Diesel & Co (derived from Titillium)

ABCDEFGHIJKLMNOPQRSTUV WXYZabcdefghijklmnopqrstu vwxyząçě0123456789(&!?$€)

THE QUICK BROWN FOX jumps over a lazy dog. Zwei Boxkämpfer jagen Eva quer durch Sylt. Lorem ipsum dolor sit amet, consectetur adipisicing elit, sed do eiusmod tempor incididunt ut labore et dolore magna aliqua. The quick brown fox jumps over a lazy dog.

Panefresco – 400wt	Chank Diesel & Co (derived from Titillium)

ABCDEFGHIJKLMNOPQRSTUV
WXYZabcdefghijklmnopqrstu
vwxyząçě0123456789(&!?$€)

THE QUICK BROWN FOX jumps over a lazy dog. Zwei Boxkämpfer jagen Eva quer durch Sylt. Lorem ipsum dolor sit amet, consectetur adipisicing elit, sed do eiusmod tempor incididunt ut labore et dolore magna aliqua. The quick brown fox jumps over a lazy dog.

Panefresco – 400wt Italic	Chank Diesel & Co (derived from Titillium)

ABCDEFGHIJKLMNOPQRSTUV
WXYZabcdefghijklmnopqrstu
vwxyząçě0123456789(&!?$€)

THE QUICK BROWN FOX jumps over a lazy dog. Zwei Boxkämpfer jagen Eva quer durch Sylt. Lorem ipsum dolor sit amet, consectetur adipisicing elit, sed do eiusmod tempor incididunt ut labore et dolore magna aliqua. The quick brown fox jumps over a lazy dog.

Panefresco – 500wt	Chank Diesel & Co (derived from Titillium)

ABCDEFGHIJKLMNOPQRSTUV
WXYZabcdefghijklmnopqrstu
vwxyząçě0123456789(&!?$€)

THE QUICK BROWN FOX jumps over a lazy dog. Zwei Boxkämpfer jagen Eva quer durch Sylt. Lorem ipsum dolor sit amet, consectetur adipisicing elit, sed do eiusmod tempor incididunt ut labore et dolore magna aliqua. The quick brown fox jumps over a lazy dog.

Panefresco – 500wt Italic	Chank Diesel & Co (derived from Titillium)

ABCDEFGHIJKLMNOPQRSTUV WXYZabcdefghijklmnopqrstu vwxyząçě0123456789(&!?$€)

THE QUICK BROWN FOX jumps over a lazy dog. Zwei Boxkämpfer jagen Eva quer durch Sylt. Lorem ipsum dolor sit amet, consectetur adipisicing elit, sed do eiusmod tempor incididunt ut labore et dolore magna aliqua. The quick brown fox jumps over a lazy dog.

Panefresco – 600wt	Chank Diesel & Co (derived from Titillium)

ABCDEFGHIJKLMNOPQRSTUV WXYZabcdefghijklmnopqrstu vwxyząçě0123456789(&!?$€)

THE QUICK BROWN FOX jumps over a lazy dog. Zwei Boxkämpfer jagen Eva quer durch Sylt. Lorem ipsum dolor sit amet, consectetur adipisicing elit, sed do eiusmod tempor incididunt ut labore et dolore magna aliqua. The quick brown fox jumps over a lazy dog.

Panefresco – 600wt Italic	Chank Diesel & Co (derived from Titillium)

ABCDEFGHIJKLMNOPQRSTUV WXYZabcdefghijklmnopqrstu vwxyząçě0123456789(&!?$€)

THE QUICK BROWN FOX jumps over a lazy dog. Zwei Boxkämpfer jagen Eva quer durch Sylt. Lorem ipsum dolor sit amet, consectetur adipisicing elit, sed do eiusmod tempor incididunt ut labore et dolore magna aliqua. The quick brown fox jumps over a lazy dog.

Panefresco – 750wt	Chank Diesel & Co (derived from Titillium)

ABCDEFGHIJKLMNOPQRSTUV
WXYZabcdefghijklmnopqrstu
vwxyząçě0123456789(&!?$€)

THE QUICK BROWN FOX jumps over a lazy dog. Zwei Boxkämpfer jagen Eva quer durch Sylt. Lorem ipsum dolor sit amet, consectetur adipisicing elit, sed do eiusmod tempor incididunt ut labore et dolore magna aliqua. The quick brown fox jumps over a lazy dog.

Panefresco – 750wt Italic	Chank Diesel & Co (derived from Titillium)

ABCDEFGHIJKLMNOPQRSTUV
WXYZabcdefghijklmnopqrstu
vwxyząçě0123456789(&!?$€)

THE QUICK BROWN FOX jumps over a lazy dog. Zwei Boxkämpfer jagen Eva quer durch Sylt. Lorem ipsum dolor sit amet, consectetur adipisicing elit, sed do eiusmod tempor incididunt ut labore et dolore magna aliqua. The quick brown fox jumps over a lazy dog.

Panefresco – 800wt	Chank Diesel & Co (derived from Titillium)

ABCDEFGHIJKLMNOPQRSTUV
WXYZabcdefghijklmnopqrstu
vwxyząçě0123456789(&!?$€)

THE QUICK BROWN FOX jumps over a lazy dog. Zwei Boxkämpfer jagen Eva quer durch Sylt. Lorem ipsum dolor sit amet, consectetur adipisicing elit, sed do eiusmod tempor incididunt ut labore et dolore magna aliqua. The quick brown fox jumps over a lazy dog.

Panefresco – 800wt Italic	Chank Diesel & Co (derived from Titillium)

ABCDEFGHIJKLMNOPQRSTUV
WXYZabcdefghijklmnopqrstu
vwxyząçě0123456789(&!?$€)

THE QUICK BROWN FOX jumps over a lazy dog. Zwei Boxkämpfer jagen Eva quer durch Sylt. Lorem ipsum dolor sit amet, consectetur adipisicing elit, sed do eiusmod tempor incididunt ut labore et dolore magna aliqua. The quick brown fox jumps over a lazy dog.

Panefresco – 999wt	Chank Diesel & Co (derived from Titillium)

ABCDEFGHIJKLMNOPQRSTUV
WXYZabcdefghijklmnopqrstu
vwxyząçě0123456789(&!?$€)

THE QUICK BROWN FOX jumps over a lazy dog. Zwei Boxkämpfer jagen Eva quer durch Sylt. Lorem ipsum dolor sit amet, consectetur adipisicing elit, sed do eiusmod tempor incididunt ut labore et dolore magna aliqua. The quick brown fox jumps over a lazy dog.

Panefresco – 999wt Italic	Chank Diesel & Co (derived from Titillium)

ABCDEFGHIJKLMNOPQRSTUV
WXYZabcdefghijklmnopqrstu
vwxyząçě0123456789(&!?$€)

THE QUICK BROWN FOX jumps over a lazy dog. Zwei Boxkämpfer jagen Eva quer durch Sylt. Lorem ipsum dolor sit amet, consectetur adipisicing elit, sed do eiusmod tempor incididunt ut labore et dolore magna aliqua. The quick brown fox jumps over a lazy dog.

Divide By Zero

fonts.tom7.com
tom7@tom7.org

32768 NO | Tom Murphy VII

The QUICK brown fox JUMPS over A lAZY

ABbCDdEeFfGgHhIiJKLlMnOPQRrS

TUVWXYZ0123456789(&:;!?$€@)

Action Jackson | Tom Murphy VII

THE FOX

ABCDEFGHIJKLMNOPQRS

TUVWXYZ0123456789(!?)

Antelope H | Tom Murphy VII

BROWN FOX

ABCDEFGHIJKLMNOPQRST

UVWXYZ0123456789(!?)

Antimony Blue	Tom Murphy VII

Quick brown fox jumps

ABCDEFGHIJKLMNOPQRSTUVWX
YZ!abcdefghijklmnopqrstuvwx
yz0123456789[:;!?]

Codon	Tom Murphy VII

BROWN FOX

ABCDEFGHIJKLMNOPQRST
UVWXYZ0123456789($!?)

Colophon	Tom Murphy VII

Brown fox

ABCDEFGHIJKLMNOPQRSTU
VWXYZabcdefghijklmnopqr
stuvwxyz0123456789(&!?$€)

Conventional Wisdom	Tom Murphy VII

OVER DOG

ABCDEFGHIJKLMNOPQR
STUVWXYZ0123456789

Cosine Katie	Tom Murphy VII

brown fox

abcdefghijklmnopq
rstuvwxyz:;!?$

Davis	Tom Murphy VII

The quick brown fox

ABCDEFGHIJKLMNOPQRSTUVW
XYZabcdefghijklmnopqrstu
vwxyz0123456789:;!?$

Doctor Azul	Tom Murphy VII

BROWN FOX

ABCDEFGHIJKLMNOPQRS

TUVWXYZ0123456789!?

Donner	Tom Murphy VII

jumps over a

abcdefghijklmnopqrs

tuvwxyz0123456789?

Douglas Adams Hand	Tom Murphy VII

LAZY DOG

ABCDEFGHIJKLMN

OPQRSTUVWXYZ!?$

Dysprosium	Tom Murphy VII

quick brown fox
jumps over a lazy dog
abcdefghijklmnopqrstuvwxyz!?

Epilog	Tom Murphy VII

Quick brown fox
ABCDEFGHIJKLMNOPQRSTU
VWXYZabcdefghijklmnopqrs
tuvwxyz0123456789(&:;!?$@)

Germs	Tom Murphy VII

BROWN FOX JUMPS
ABCDEFGHIJKLMNOPQRS
TUVWXYZ(&!?$@)

Guild of Professional Actors	Tom Murphy VII

the brown fox over a lazy dog

abcdefghijklmnopqrstuvwxyz

Hokey is Lif	Tom Murphy VII

Fox jumps over a lazy dog

ABCDEFGHIJKLMNOPQRSTUVWX
YZabcdefghijklmnopqrstuvwxyzäç
é0123456789(&:;!?$€@)

I Suck At Golf	Tom Murphy VII

fox dog

abcdefghijklmnopqrstuv
wxyz0123456789(&:;!?$@)

Levity	Tom Murphy VII

Quick brown fox

ABCDEFGHIJKLMNOPQRSTUV
wxyzabcdefghijklmnopqrstu
vwxyz0123456789[:;!?$@]

Lexographer	Tom Murphy VII

QUICK BROWN

ABCDEFGHIJKLMNOPQRS
TUVWXYZ0123456789&

Linear	Tom Murphy VII

the brown fox

abcdefghijklmn
opqrstuvwxyz

Melaine | Tom Murphy VII

the quick brown fox jumps over a

abcdefghijklmnopqrstuvwxyz

Meta Language | Tom Murphy VII

QUICK BROWN FOX JUMPS

ABCDEFGHIJKLMNOPQRSTUV
WXYZ0123456789(;:!?$€@)

Music | Tom Murphy VII

the brown
lazy dog

abcdefghijklm
nopqrstuvwxy
z0123456789(:;,./-

Non Blocking Socket | Tom Murphy VII

Quick brown fox

ABCDEFGHIJKLMNOPQRSTUVW
XYZabcdefghijklmnopqrstuvw
xyzäçé0123456789(&:;!?$¥€)

Null Pointer | Tom Murphy VII

quick fox

abcdefghijklmnopqrs
tuvwxyz0123456789!?

One Constant | Tom Murphy VII

THE BROWN FOX

ABCDEFGHIjKLMNOPQRSTUV
WXYZ0123456789(&:;!?$€)

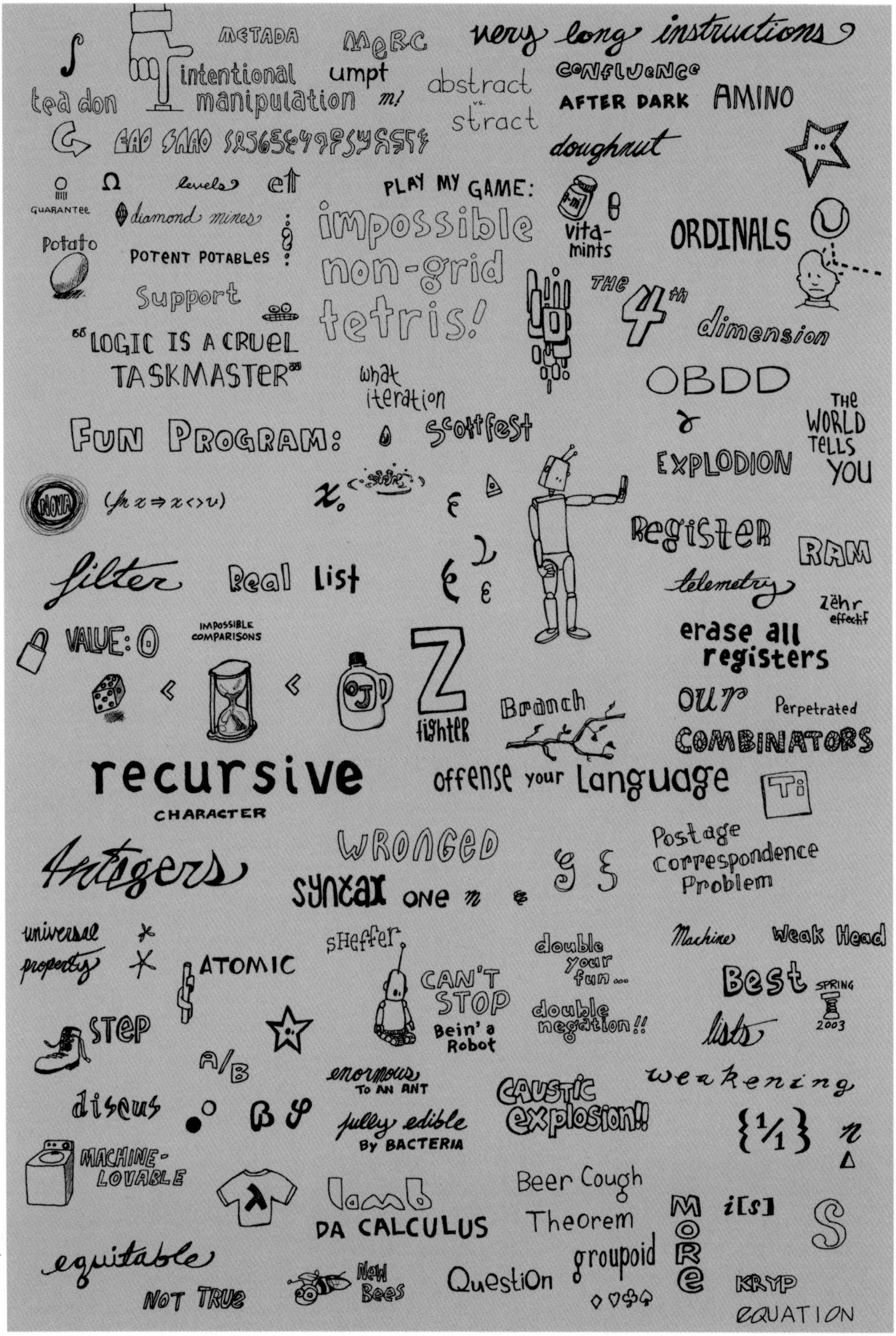

Sketches from various notebooks. © 2012 Tom Murphy VII | Divide By Zero

Optic.bot | Tom Murphy VII

Quick fox

ABCDEFGHIJKLMNOPQRST
UVWXYZabcdefghijklmno
pqrstuvwxyz0123456789

Prog.bot | Tom Murphy VII

Quick fox

ABCDEFGHIJKLMNOPQRST
UVWXYZabcdefghijklmno
pqrstuvwxyz0123456789

Pinball Data | Tom Murphy VII

FOX DOG

ABCDEFGHIJKLMNOPQR
STUVWXYZ0123456789

Potassium Scandal | Tom Murphy VII

QUICK BROWN FOX
JUMPS OVER A

ABCDEFGHIJKLMNOPQR
STUWXYZ0123456789&

Proteron | Tom Murphy VII

jumps over a

abcdefghijklmnopqrst
uvwxyz0123456789!?

Real Bttsoief | Tom Murphy VII

quick brown
jumps over a lazy

abcdefghijklmnopqrs
tuvwxyz0123456789!?@

Resurgence	Tom Murphy VII

jumps over a

abcdefghijklmnopqrstu

vwxyz0123456789(:;!?)

Robot Teacher	Tom Murphy VII

The quick brown fox

ABCDEFGHIJKLMNOPQRSTUV

WXYZabcdefghijklmnopqrst

uvwxyz0123456789(&:;!?$@)

Signal To Noise	Tom Murphy VII

the quick brown fox jumps over

quick brown fox jumps over a lazy

abcdefghijklmnopqrstuvwxyzabcdefghijklmnopqrstuvwxyz

Tetanus	Tom Murphy VII

The quick brown fox jumps over a lazy dog

ABCDEFGHIJKLMNOPQRSTUVWXYZabc
defghijklmnopqrstuvwxyz0123456789

This Boring Party	Tom Murphy VII

Quick brown fox jumps

ABCDEFGHIJKLMNOPQRSTUVWXY
Zabcdefghijklmnopqrstuvwxyz
0123456789(&.:;!?$€£¥@)

Toast	Tom Murphy VII

QUICK BROWN
FOX JUMPS

ABCDEFGHIJKLMNOPQRSTUVWXYZ

Tom's Handwriting | Tom Murphy VII

Quick brown fox

ABCDEFGHIJKLMNOPQRSTUV
WXYZabcdefghijklmnopqrstu
vwxyz0123456789(&:;!?$¢@)

Tom's New Roman | Tom Murphy VII

Quick brown fox

ABCDEFGHIJKLMNOPQRSTUV
WXYZabcdefghijklmnopqrstu
vwxyzäçé0123456789(&:;!?$¢£)

Tombats (selection) | Tom Murphy VII

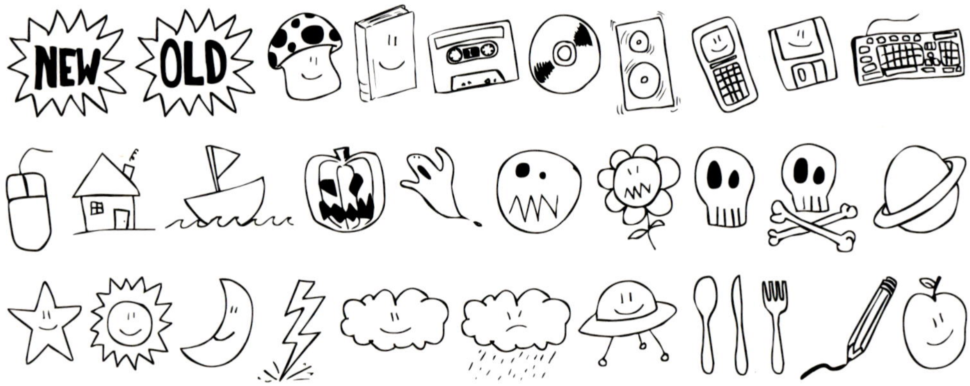

Tombats 3 (selection)	Tom Murphy VII

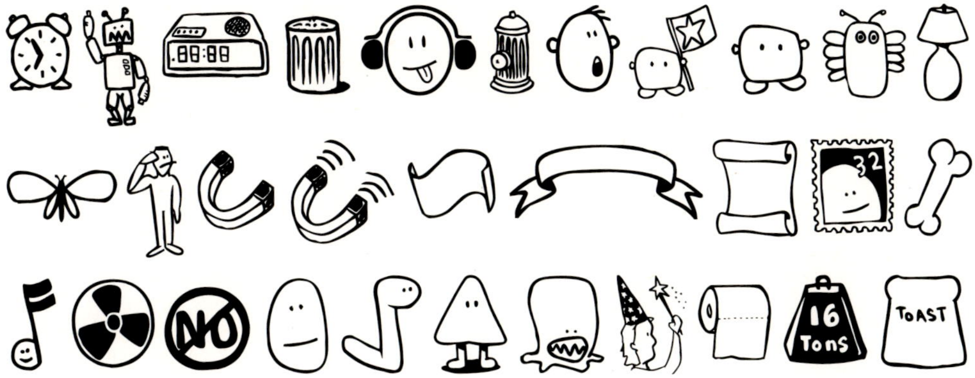

Tombats 4 (selection)	Tom Murphy VII

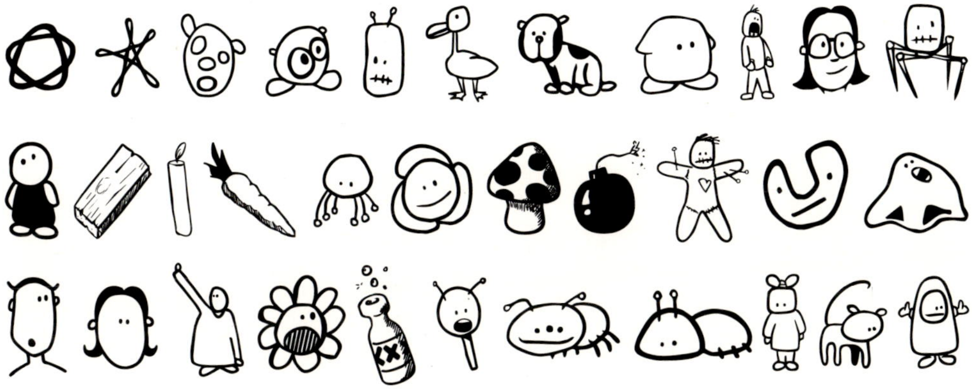

Tombats 6 (selection)	Tom Murphy VII

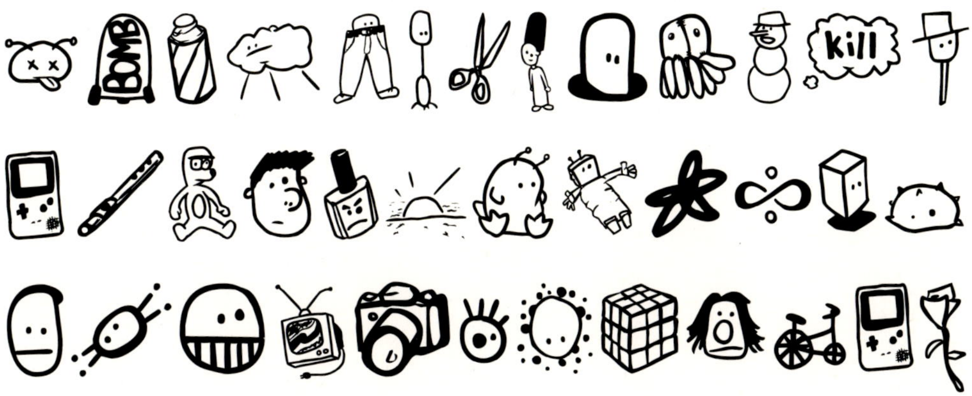

Tombats 7 (selection) | Tom Murphy VII

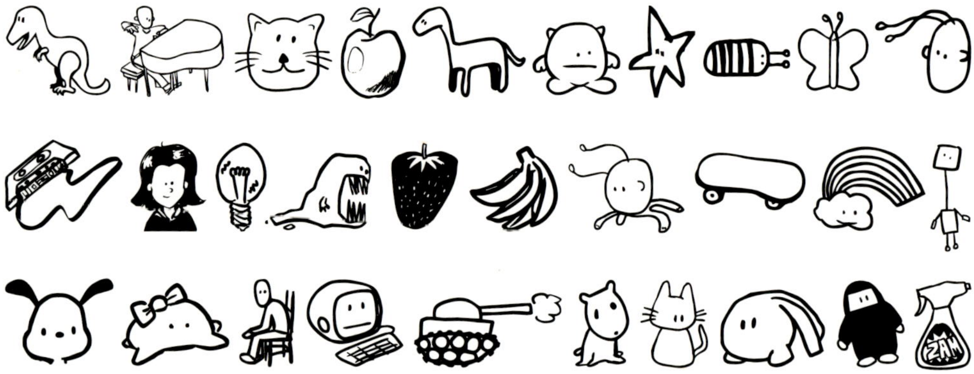

Tombats Smiles (selection) | Tom Murphy VII

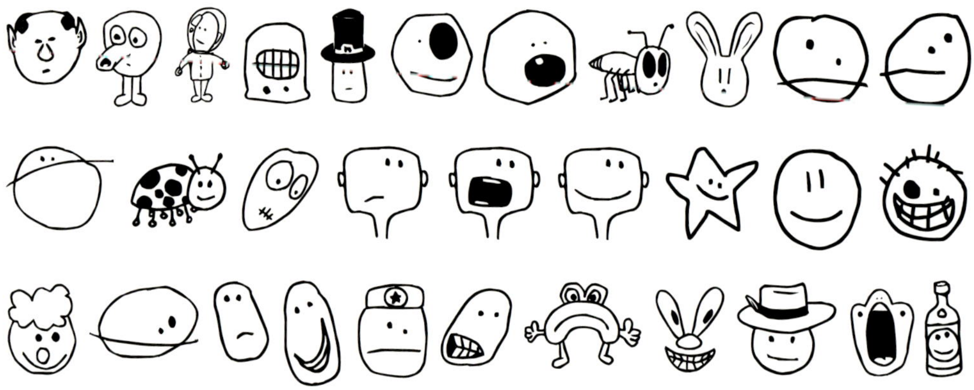

Tombots (selection) | Tom Murphy VII

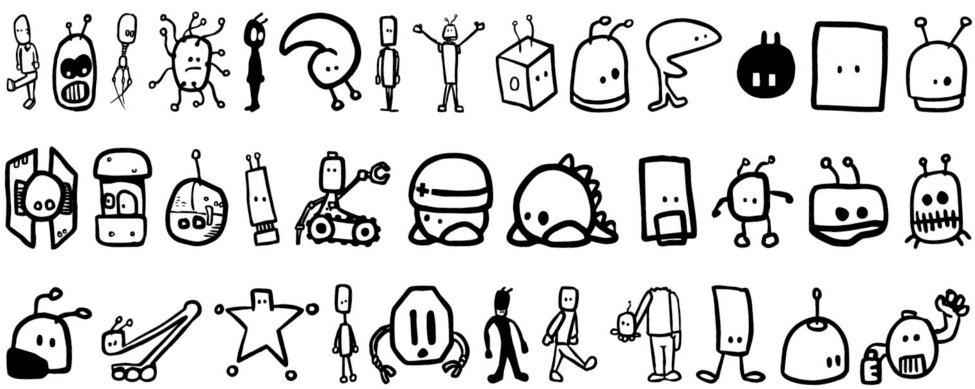

Tommy's First Alphabet	Tom Murphy VII

THE DOG FOX JUMPS OVER

ABCDEFGHIJKLMNOPQRSTUVWXYZ

Tuesday	Tom Murphy VII

brown fox

abcdefghijklmnopqrstu
vwxyz0123456789(!?$)

Two Turtle Doves	Tom Murphy VII

THE BROWN

ABCDEFGHIJKLMNOPQRSTUVWXYZabcdefg
hijklmnopqrstuvwxyz0123456789(&!?$@)

Wolves, Lower	Tom Murphy VII

QUICK BROWN FOX

ABCDEFGHIJKLMNOPQRSTUVWXYZ abcde
fghijklmnopqrstuvwxyz0123456789&

Yikatu	Tom Murphy VII

QUICK FOX

abcdefghijklmnopqrst
uvwxyz0123456789?

Zinc Boomerang	Tom Murphy VII

QUICK BROWN FOX
OVER A LAZY

ABCDEFGHIJKLMNOPQRS
TUVWXYZ0123456789&!?$

Fontfabric

fontfabric.com
fontfabric@gmail.com

Age	Svetoslav Simov

Quick brown

ABCDEFGHIJKLMNOPQRSTUV
WXYZabcdefghijklmnopqr
stuvwxyzäçé0123456789!?

Code – Light	Svetoslav Simov

THE DOG

ABCDEFGHIJKLMNOPQRST
UVWXYZÄÇÉ0123456789!?

Code – Bold	Svetoslav Simov

THE DOG

ABCDEFGHIJKLMNOPQRST
UVWXYZÄÇÉ0123456789!?

Dan | Svetoslav Simov

Brown Fox

ABCDEFGHIJKLMNOPQRSTUVWX
YZabcdefghijklmnopqrstuvw
xyzäçé0123456789(&:;!?$№°)
АБВГДЕЁЖЗИЙКЛМНОПРСТУФХ
ЦЧШЩЪЫЬЭЮЯабвгдеёжзийк
лмнопрстуфхцчшщъыьэюя

Dekar – Light | Svetoslav Simov

ABCDEFGHIJKLMNOPQRSTUVWX
YZabcdefghijklmnopqrstuvwxyz
äçé0123456789(!?€)

THE QUICK BROWN FOX jumps over a lazy dog. Zwei Boxkämpfer jagen Eva quer durch Sylt. Lorem ipsum dolor sit amet, consectetur adipisicing elit, sed do eiusmod tempor incididunt ut labore et dolore magna aliqua. The quick brown fox jumps over a lazy dog. Zwei Boxkämpfer jagen Eva quer

Dekar – Regular | Svetoslav Simov

ABCDEFGHIJKLMNOPQRSTUVWX
YZabcdefghijklmnopqrstuvwxyz
zäçé0123456789(!?€)

THE QUICK BROWN FOX jumps over a lazy dog. Zwei Boxkämpfer jagen Eva quer durch Sylt. Lorem ipsum dolor sit amet, consectetur adipisicing elit, sed do eiusmod tempor incididunt ut labore et dolore magna aliqua. The quick brown fox jumps over a lazy dog. Zwei Boxkämpfer jagen Eva quer

Gota – Light | Svetoslav Simov

BROWN FOX

AaBCDEeFGHIJJKLM
NOPQRSTtUVWXYyZÄ
ÇÉ0123456789!?

Gota – Regular | Svetoslav Simov

a lazy dog

AaBCDEeFGHIJJKLMN
OPQRSTtUVWXYyZÄÇÉ
0123456789!?

Hero – Light | Svetoslav Simov

ABCDEFGHIJKLMNOPQRST
UVWXYZabcdefghijklmnop
qrstuvwxyzäçé0123456789&

THE QUICK BROWN FOX jumps over a lazy dog. Zwei Boxkämpfer jagen Eva quer durch Sylt. Lorem ipsum dolor sit amet, consectetur adipisicing elit, sed do eiusmod tempor incididunt ut labore et dolore magna aliqua. The quick

Hero – Regular | Svetoslav Simov

ABCDEFGHIJKLMNOPQRST
UVWXYZabcdefghijklmnop
qrstuvwxyzäçé0123456789&

THE QUICK BROWN FOX jumps over a lazy dog. Zwei Boxkämpfer jagen Eva quer durch Sylt. Lorem ipsum dolor sit amet, consectetur adipisicing elit, sed do eiusmod tempor incididunt ut labore et dolore magna aliqua. The quick

Null | Svetoslav Simov

Brown fox

ABCDEFGHIJKLMNOPQRSTU
VWXYZabcdefghijklmnopqr
stuvwxyzäçé0123456789

Rex	Svetoslav Simov

BROWN FOX JUMPS OVER

Light

ABCDEFGHIJKLMNOPQRSTUVWX
YZABCDEFGHIJKLMNOPQRSTUVW
XYZÄÇÉ0123456789&!?
АБВГДЕЁЖЗИЙКЛМНОПРСТУФХЦ
ЧШЩЪЫЬЭЮЯАБВГДЕЁЖЗИЙКЛМ
НОПРСТУФХЦЧШЩЪЫЬЭЮЯ

Bold

ABCDEFGHIJKLMNOPQRSTUVW
XYZABCDEFGHIJKLMNOPQRSTU
VWXYZÄÇÉ0123456789&!?

Bold Inline

ABCDEFGHIJKLMNOPQRSTUVW
XYZABCDEFGHIJKLMNOPQRSTU
VWXYZÄÇÉ0123456789&!?

THE QUICK
BROWN
FOX JUMPS OVER
A LAZY DOG
ZWEI BOXKÄMPFER
JAGEN EVA

SAF	Svetoslav Simov

THE DOG

ABCDEFGHIJKLMNOPQRST
UVWXYZÄÇÉ0123456789

Intro – Regular	Svetoslav Simov

QUICK BROWN
LAZY DOG

ABCDEFGHIJKLMNO
PQRSTUVWXYZÄÇÉ
0123456789&:;!?
АБВГДЕЁЖЗИЙКЛМ
НОПРСТУФХЦЧШЩ
ЪЫЬЭЮЯАБ

Intro – Inline	Svetoslav Simov

QUICK BROWN
LAZY DOG

ABCDEFGHIJKLMNO
PQRSTUVWXYZÄÇÉ
0123456789&:;!?
АБВГДЕЁЖЗИЙКЛМ
НОПРСТУФХЦЧШЩ
ЪЫЬЭЮЯАБ

Val – Stencil	Svetoslav Simov

BROWN FOX

ABCDEFGHIJKLMNO
PQRSTUVWXYZÄÇÉ
0123456789(&:;!?$£¥€)

Weston – Light | Pavel Pavlov

FOX JUMPS OVER
ABCDEFGHIJKLMNO
PQRSTUVWXYZÄÇÉ
0123456789!?

Weston – Regular | Pavel Pavlov

FOX JUMPS OVER
ABCDEFGHIJKLMNO
PQRSTUVWXYZÄÇÉ
0123456789!?

Friedrich Althausen

friedrichalthausen.de
post@friedrichalthausen.de

Friedrich Althausen | friedrichalthausen.de

Vollkorn – Regular	Friedrich Althausen

ABCDEFGHIJKLMNOPQRSTU VWXYZabcdefghijklmnopqrst uvwxyzäçé0123456789(&:;!?$€)

THE QUICK BROWN FOX jumps over a lazy dog. Zwei Boxkämpfer jagen Eva quer durch Sylt. Lorem ipsum dolor sit amet, consectetur adipisicing elit, sed do eiusmod tempor incididunt ut labore et dolore magna aliqua. The quick brown fox jumps over

Vollkorn – Italic	Friedrich Althausen

ABCDEFGHIJKLMNOPQRSTUV WXYZabcdefghijklmnopqrstuvwxy zäçé0123456789(&:;!?$¢£¥€@)

THE QUICK BROWN FOX jumps over a lazy dog. Zwei Boxkämpfer jagen Eva quer durch Sylt. Lorem ipsum dolor sit amet, consectetur adipisicing elit, sed do eiusmod tempor incididunt ut labore et dolore magna aliqua. The quick brown fox jumps over a lazy dog. Zwei Boxkämpfer jagen Eva

Vollkorn – Bold	Friedrich Althausen

ABCDEFGHIJKLMNOPQRST UVWXYZabcdefghijklmnop qrstuvwxyzäçé0123456789&

THE QUICK BROWN FOX jumps over a lazy dog. Zwei Boxkämpfer jagen Eva quer durch Sylt. Lorem ipsum dolor sit amet, consectetur adipisicing elit, sed do eiusmod tempor incididunt ut labore et dolore magna aliqua. The

The quick
BROWN
fox jumps over
over a lazy
DOG
Zwei Boxkämpfer

Friedrich Althausen | friedrichalthausen.de

ABCDEFGHIJKLMNOPQRST UVWXYZabcdefghijklmnopq rstuvwxyzäçé0123456789&€

THE QUICK BROWN FOX jumps over a lazy dog. Zwei Boxkämpfer jagen Eva quer durch Sylt. Lorem ipsum dolor sit amet, consectetur adipisicing elit, sed do eiusmod tempor incididunt ut labore et dolore magna aliqua. The quick brown

Gluk

glukfonts.pl
gluksza@wp.pl

Foglihten – Regular	Gluk

Brown fox

ABCDEFGHIJKKLMNOPQQRRS
TUVWXYZabcdefghijklmnopq
rstuvwxyząçě0123456789(&:;!?€)
ABCDEFGHIJKLMNOPQRSTUVW
XYZĄÇĚ0123456789(&!?$€@)

Foglihten – Black Petite Caps	Gluk

LAZY

ABCDEFGHIJKLMN
OPQRSTUVWXYZĄÇ
Ě0123456789(&:;!?€)
АБВГДЕЁЖЗИЙКЛ
МНОПРСТУФХЦЧ
ШЩЪЫЬЭЮЯАБ

Foglihten – Petite Caps | Gluk

LAZY DOG

ABCDEFGHIJKLMNOPQRSTUV
WXYZABCDEFGHIJKLMNOPQRSTU
VWXYZĄÇĔ0123456789(&:;!?$£¥€@)

Foglihten No01 | Gluk

FOX

ABCDEFGHIJKKLMNOPQQRR
STUVWXYZĄÇĔ0123456789$€

Foglihten No03 | Gluk

FOX

ABCDEFGHIJKKLMNOPQQRR
STUVWXYZĄÇĔ0123456789$€

Foglihten Fr01	Gluk

OVER A LAZY

ABCDEFGHIJKLMNOPQRSTUV
WXYZĄÇĚ0123456789&.:;!?$£¥€

Foglihten Fr02	Gluk

JUMPS OVER

ABCDEFGHIJKLMNOPQRSTUV
WXYZĄÇĚ0123456789&.:;!?$£¥€

Foglihten – DeH02, DeH04 (selection)	Gluk

Mikodacs	Gluk

Fox jumps over

ABCDEFGHIJKLMNOPQRSTUVWXYZ

abcdefghijklmnopqrstuvwxyząçĕ

0123456789(&:;,!?$¢£¥€@)

АБВГДЕЁЖЗИЙКЛМНОПРСТУФХЦЧ

ШЩЪЫЬЭЮЯабвгдеёжзийклмно

прстуфхцчшщъыьэюя

Mikodacs – Petite Caps	Gluk

BROWN FOX

ABCDEFGHIJKLMNOPQRSTUVWXYZ

ABCDEFGHIJKLMNOPQRSTUVWXYZĄ

ÇĔ0123456789(&:;,!?$¢£¥€)

АБВГДЕЁЖЗИЙКЛМНОПРСТУФХЦЧ

ШЩЪЫЬЭЮЯАБВГДЕЁЖЗИЙКЛМН

ОПРСТУФХЦЧШЩЪЫЬЭЮЯ

Rawengulk – Ultra Light	Gluk

ABCDEFGHIJKLMNOPQRSTUV
WXYZabcdefghijklmnopqrstuv
wxyząçě0123456789(&:;!?$¢£¥€)

THE QUICK BROWN FOX jumps over a lazy dog. Zwei Boxkämpfer jagen Eva quer durch Sylt. Lorem ipsum dolor sit amet, consectetur adipisicing elit, sed do eiusmod tempor incididunt ut labore et dolore magna aliqua. The quick brown fox jumps over a lazy dog.

Rawengulk – Light	Gluk

ABCDEFGHIJKLMNOPQRSTUV
WXYZabcdefghijklmnopqrstuv
wxyząçě0123456789(&:;!?$¢£¥€)

THE QUICK BROWN FOX jumps over a lazy dog. Zwei Boxkämpfer jagen Eva quer durch Sylt. Lorem ipsum dolor sit amet, consectetur adipisicing elit, sed do eiusmod tempor incididunt ut labore et dolore magna aliqua. The quick brown fox jumps over

Rawengulk – Regular	Gluk

ABCDEFGHIJKLMNOPQRSTU
VWXYZabcdefghijklmnopqrst
uvwxyząçě0123456789(&:;!?$€)

THE QUICK BROWN FOX jumps over a lazy dog. Zwei Boxkämpfer jagen Eva quer durch Sylt. Lorem ipsum dolor sit amet, consectetur adipisicing elit, sed do eiusmod tempor incididunt ut labore et dolore magna aliqua. The quick brown fox jumps over

Rawengulk – Petite Caps	Gluk

ABCDEFGHIJKLMNOPQRSTU VWXYZABCDEFGHIJKLMNOPQRSTU VWXYZĄÇĚ0123456789(&:;!?$¢£¥€@)

THE QUICK BROWN FOX JUMPS OVER A LAZY DOG. ZWEI BOXKÄMPFER JAGEN EVA QUER DURCH SYLT. LOREM IPSUM DOLOR SIT AMET, CONSECTETUR ADIPISICING ELIT, SED DO EIUSMOD TEMPOR INCIDIDUNT UT LABORE ET DOLORE MAGNA ALIQUA. THE QUICK BROWN FOX JUMPS OVER A LAZY DOG.

Rawengulk – Demi Bold	Gluk

ABCDEFGHIJKLMNOPQRSTU VWXYZabcdefghijklmnopqrst uvwxyząçě0123456789(&:;!?$€)

THE QUICK BROWN FOX jumps over a lazy dog. Zwei Boxkämpfer jagen Eva quer durch Sylt. Lorem ipsum dolor sit amet, consectetur adipisicing elit, sed do eius-mod tempor incididunt ut labore et dolore magna aliqua. The quick brown fox

Rawengulk – Bold	Gluk

ABCDEFGHIJKLMNOPQRSTU VWXYZabcdefghijklmnopqrst uvwxyząçě0123456789(&:;!?$€)

THE QUICK BROWN FOX jumps over a lazy dog. Zwei Boxkämpfer jagen Eva quer durch Sylt. Lorem ipsum dolor sit amet, consectetur adipisicing elit, sed do ei-usmod tempor incididunt ut labore et dolore magna aliqua. The quick brown fox

Opattfram 01 (selection)	Gluk

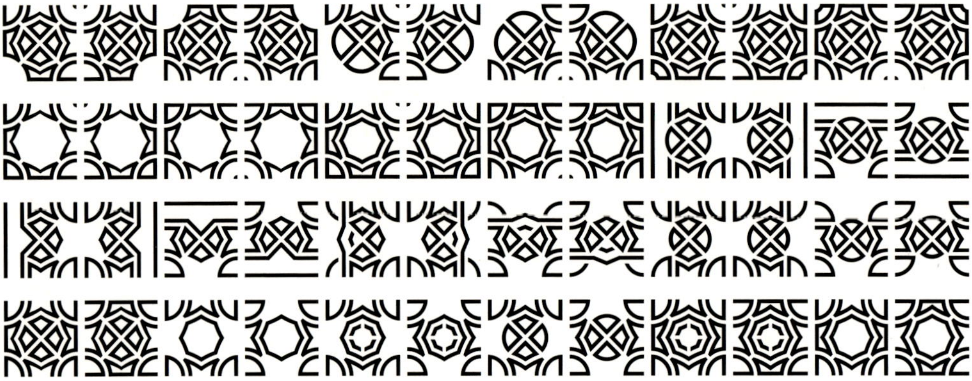

Qumpellka No12	Gluk

The quick brown

ABCDEFGHIJKLMNOPQRS
TUVWXYZabcdefghijklmnopq
rstuvwxyząçě0123456789&№

Reswysokr	Gluk

The fox jumps

ABCDEFGHIJKLMNOPQRSTUVWXYZabcde
fghijklmnopqrstuvwxyząçě0123456789€

Resagnicto – Regular	Gluk

ABCDEFGHIJKLMNOPQRSTUV
WXYZabcdefghijklmnopqrst
uvwxyząçě0123456789(&!?€)

THE QUICK BROWN FOX jumps over a lazy dog. Zwei Boxkämpfer jagen Eva quer durch Sylt. Lorem ipsum dolor sit amet, consectetur adipisic-ing elit, sed do eiusmod tempor incididunt ut labore et dolore magna

Resagnicto – Italic	Gluk

ABCDEFGHIJKLMNOPQRSTUV
WXYZabcdefghijklmnopqrst
uvwxyząçě0123456789(&!?€)

THE QUICK BROWN FOX jumps over a lazy dog. Zwei Boxkämpfer ja-gen Eva quer durch Sylt. Lorem ipsum dolor sit amet, consectetur adipisicing elit, sed do eiusmod tempor incididunt ut labore et do-

Resagnicto – Bold	Gluk

ABCDEFGHIJKLMNOPQRSTU
VWXYZabcdefghijklmnopq
rstuvwxyząçě0123456789&

THE QUICK BROWN FOX jumps over a lazy dog. Zwei Boxkämpfer jagen Eva quer durch Sylt. Lorem ipsum dolor sit amet, consecte-tur adipisicing elit, sed do eiusmod tempor incididunt ut labore et

Resagokr – Light	Gluk

ABCDEFGHIJKLMNOPQRSTUVWXYZ
abcdefghijklmnopqrstuvwxyząçě
0123456789(&:;!?$¢£¥€@)
АБВГДЕЁЖЗИЙКЛМНОПРСТУФХЦ
ЧШЩЪЫЬЭЮЯабвгдеёжзийклмно
прстуфхцчшщъыьэюя

THE QUICK BROWN FOX jumps over a lazy dog. Zwei Boxkämpfer jagen Eva quer durch Sylt. Lorem ipsum dolor sit amet, consectetur adipisicing elit, sed do eiusmod tempor incididunt ut labore et dolore magna aliqua. The quick brown fox jumps over a lazy dog. Zwei Boxkämpfer

Resagokr – Regular	Gluk

ABCDEFGHIJKLMNOPQRSTUVWX
YZabcdefghijklmnopqrstuvwxyz
ąçě0123456789(&:;!?$¢£¥€@)
АБВГДЕЁЖЗИЙКЛМНОПРСТУФХ
ЦЧШЩЪЫЬЭЮЯабвгдеёжзийклм
нопрстуфхцчшщъыьэюя

THE QUICK BROWN FOX jumps over a lazy dog. Zwei Boxkämpfer jagen Eva quer durch Sylt. Lorem ipsum dolor sit amet, consectetur adipisicing elit, sed do eiusmod tempor incididunt ut labore et dolore magna aliqua. The quick brown fox jumps over a lazy dog.

Resagokr – Bold	Gluk

ABCDEFGHIJKLMNOPQRSTUVW
XYZabcdefghijklmnopqrstuvw
xyząçě0123456789(&:;!?$¢£¥€)
АБВГДЕЁЖЗИЙКЛМНОПРСТУФ
ХЦЧШЩЪЫЬЭЮЯабвгдеёжзий
клмнопрстуфхцчшщъыьэюя

THE QUICK BROWN FOX jumps over a lazy dog. Zwei Boxkämpfer jagen Eva quer durch Sylt. Lorem ipsum dolor sit amet, consectetur adipisicing elit, sed do eiusmod tempor incididunt ut labore et dolore magna aliqua. The quick brown fox

Zantroke	Gluk

The fox

ABCDEFGHIJKLMNOPQRSTUVWX
YZabcdefghijklmnopqrstuvwxy
ząçě0123456789(&:;!?$¢£¥€@)
АБВГДЕЁЖЗИЙКЛМНОПРСТУФХ
ЦЧШЩЪЫЬЭЮЯабвгдеёжзийк
лмнопрстуфхцчшщъыьэюя

BROWN

ABCDEFGHIJKKLMNOPQQ
RRSTUVVWXYZabcdefghijk
lmnopqrstuvwxyząçě
0123456789(&.,:;!?$¢£¥€@)

ABCDEFGHIJKKLMNOPQQRRSTUV
WXYZ0123456789(&.,:;!?$€@)

АБВГДЕЁЖЗИЙКЛМНОП
РСТУФХЦЧШЩЪЫЬЭЮЯаб
вгдеёжзийклмнопрстуфх
цчшщъыьэюя

The quick
brown
fox jumps over
a lazy dog
ZWEI
Boxkämpfer jagen

BROWN

ABCDEFGHIJKLMNOPQRR
STUVWXYZabcdefghijklm
nopqrstuvwxyząçě
0123456789(&:;!?$¢£¥€@)
АБВГДЕЁЖЗИЙКЛМНОП
РСТУФХЦЧШЩЪЫЬЭЮЯаб
вгдеёжзийклмнопрстуф
хцчшщъыьэюя

Jovanny Lemonad

jovanny.ru
lemonad@jovanny.ru

Bender	Creatica & Ivan Gladkikh

Fox jumps over a lazy dog

Regular

ABCDEFGHIJKLMNOPQRSTUVWXY
Zabcdefghijklmnopqrstuvwxyząçě
0123456789(&.;:!?$¢¥€@№)
АБВГДЕЁЖЗИЙКЛМНОПРСТУФХЦ
ЧШЩЪЫЬЭЮЯабвгдеёжзийклмн
опрстуфхцчшщъыьэюя

Italic

ABCDEFGHIJKLMNOPQRSTUVWXY
Zabcdefghijklmnopqrstuvwxyząçě
0123456789(&.;:!?$¢¥€@№)

Light

ABCDEFGHIJKLMNOPQRSTUVWXY
Zabcdefghijklmnopqrstuvwxyząçě
0123456789(&.;:!?$¢¥€@№)

Light Italic

ABCDEFGHIJKLMNOPQRSTUVWXY Zabcdefghijklmnopqrstuvwxyząçě 0123456789(&:;!?$¢¥€@№)

Bold

ABCDEFGHIJKLMNOPQRSTUVWX YZabcdefghijklmnopqrstuvwxyz ąçě0123456789(&:;!?$¢¥€@№)

Bold Italic

ABCDEFGHIJKLMNOPQRSTUVWX YZabcdefghijklmnopqrstuvwxyz ąçě0123456789(&:;!?$¢¥€@№)

Black

ABCDEFGHIJKLMNOPQRSTUVW XYZabcdefghijklmnopqrstuvwx yząçě0123456789(&!?$¥€@№)

Black Italic

ABCDEFGHIJKLMNOPQRSTUVW XYZabcdefghijklmnopqrstuvwx yząçě0123456789(&:;!?$€@№)

20 DB	Ivan Gladkikh

The fox

ABCDEFGHIJKLMNOPQR
STUVWXYZabcdefghijklm
nopqrstuvwxyz0123456
789АБВГДЕЁЖЗИЙКЛМ
НОПРСТУФХЦЧШЩЪЫЬ
ЭЮЯабвгдеёжзийклмн
опрстуфхцчшщъыьэюя

Airport	Stefan Vanli

BROWN FOX OVER

ABCDEFGHIJKLMNOPQRSTUVWXYZabc
defghijKLMNOPQRSTUVWXYZ0123456
789(&:;,!?$€@№)АБВГДЕЁЖЗИЙКЛМ
НОПРСТУФХЦЧШЩЪЫЬЭЮЯабвгдеё
ЖЗИЙКЛМНОПРСТУФХЦЧШЩЪЫЬЭЮЯ

Bicubik	Treks

BROWN FOX JUMPS OVER A

ABCDEFGHIJKLMNOP
QRSTUVWXYZ012345
6789(&:;!?$€@№)АБВГ
ДЕЁЖЗИЙКЛМНОПРС
ТУФХЦЧШЩЪЫЬЭЮЯ

Days	Merlinni & Aleksey Maslov

Quick brown fox jumps over a

ABCDEFGHIJKLMNOPQRSTU
VWXYZabcdefghijklmnopqrstu
vwxyzäçě0123456789&!?€АБ
ВГДЕЁЖЗИЙКЛМНОПРСТУФ
ХЦЧШЩЪЫЬЭЮЯабвгдеёжзи
йклмнопрстуфхцчшщъыьэюя

Cuprum – Regular | Ivan Gladkikh

ABCDEFGHIJKLMNOPQRSTUVWX
YZabcdefghijklmnopqrstuvwxyzą
çé0123456789(&:;!?$¢£¥€@№)
АБВГДЕЁЖЗИЙКЛМНОПРСТУФХ
ЦЧШЩЪЫЬЭЮЯабвгдеёжзийкл
мнопрстуфхцчшщъыьэюя

THE QUICK BROWN FOX jumps over a lazy dog. Zwei Boxkämpfer jagen Eva quer durch Sylt. Lorem ipsum dolor sit amet, consectetur adipisicing elit, sed do eiusmod tempor incididunt ut labore et dolore magna aliqua. The quick brown fox jumps over a lazy dog. Zwei Boxkämpfer jagen Eva quer

Cuprum – Italic | Ivan Gladkikh

ABCDEFGHIJKLMNOPQRSTUVWX
YZabcdefghijklmnopqrstuvwxyzą
çé0123456789(&:;!?$¢£¥€@№)
АБВГДЕЁЖЗИЙКЛМНОПРСТУФХ
ЦЧШЩЪЫЬЭЮЯабвгдеёжзийкл
мнопрстуфхцчшщъыьэюя

THE QUICK BROWN FOX jumps over a lazy dog. Zwei Boxkämpfer jagen Eva quer durch Sylt. Lorem ipsum dolor sit amet, consectetur adipisicing elit, sed do eiusmod tempor incididunt ut labore et dolore magna aliqua. The quick brown fox jumps over a lazy dog. Zwei Boxkämpfer jagen Eva quer

Cuprum – Bold	Ivan Gladkikh

ABCDEFGHIJKLMNOPQRSTUVW XYZabcdefghijklmnopqrstuvw xyząçé0123456789(&:;!?$£¥€№) АБВГДЕЁЖЗИЙКЛМНОПРСТУФ ХЦЧШЩЪЫЬЭЮЯабвгдеёжзий клмнопрстуфхцчшщъыьэюя

THE QUICK BROWN FOX jumps over a lazy dog. Zwei Boxkämpfer jagen Eva quer durch Sylt. Lorem ipsum dolor sit amet, consectetur adipisicing elit, sed do eiusmod tempor incididunt ut labore et dolore magna aliqua. The quick brown fox jumps over a lazy dog. Zwei Boxkämpfer

Cuprum – Bold Italic	Ivan Gladkikh

ABCDEFGHIJKLMNOPQRSTUVW XYZabcdefghijklmnopqrstuvw xyząçé0123456789(&:;!?$£¥€№) АБВГДЕЁЖЗИЙКЛМНОПРСТУФ ХЦЧШЩЪЫЬЭЮЯабвгдеёжзий клмнопрстуфхцчшщъыьэюя

THE QUICK BROWN FOX jumps over a lazy dog. Zwei Boxkämpfer jagen Eva quer durch Sylt. Lorem ipsum dolor sit amet, consectetur adipisicing elit, sed do eiusmod tempor incididunt ut labore et dolore magna aliqua. The quick brown fox jumps over a lazy dog. Zwei Boxkämpfer

Dited	Creatica

The quick brown
jumps over a lazy dog

ABCDEFGHIJKLMNOPQRSTUVWXYZa
bcdefghijklmnopqrstuvwxyz0123
456789(&.:;!?)АБВГДЕЁЖЗИЙКЛМНО
ПРСТУФХЦЧШЩЪЫЬЭЮЯабвгдеёж
зийклмнопрстуфхцчшщъыьэюя

Epool	Éti-design

brown fox

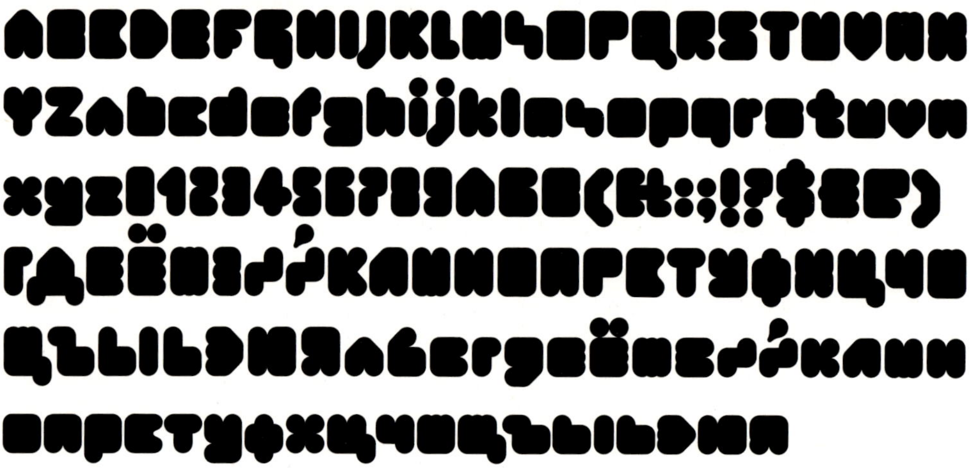

Flow – Regular	Andartem

The quick brown fox jumps over a lazy dog

ABCDEFGHIJKLMNOPQRSTUVWXYZ abcdefghijklmnopqrstuvwxyz012345 6789(&:;!?€)АБВГДЕЁЖЗИЙКЛМНО ПРСТУФХЦЧШЩЪЫЬЭЮЯабвгдеё жзийклмнопрстуфхцчшщъыьэюя

Flow – Bold	Andartem

The quick brown fox jumps over a lazy dog

ABCDEFGHIJKLMNOPQRSTUVWXYZ abcdefghijklmnopqrstuvwxyz012345 6789(&:;!?€)АБВГДЕЁЖЗИЙКЛМНО ПРСТУФХЦЧШЩЪЫЬЭЮЯабвгдеё жзийклмнопрстуфхцчшщъыьэюя

Jovanny Lemonad | jovanny.ru

Furore	Pouzeot

BROWN
FOX JUMPS OVER
ABCDEFGHIJKLMNOPQRST
UVWXYZ0123456789&:;!?€
АБВГДЕЁЖЗИЙКЛМНОПРС
ТУФХЦЧШЩЪЫЬЭЮЯ

Hardpixel	Treks

Brown Fox
ABCDEFGHIJKLMNOPQRSTUVW
XYZabcdefghijklmnopqrstuv
wxyz0123456789(&:;!?$€)АБВ
ГДЕЁЖЗИЙКЛМНОПРСТУФХЦЧ
ШЩЪЫЬЭЮЯабвгдеёжзийкл
мнопрстуфхцчшщъыьэюя

Hattori Hanzo – Light	Roman Shamin & Ivan Gladkikh

ABCDEFGHIJKLMNOPQRSTUVWX
YZabcdefghijklmnopqrstuvwxyz
0123456789(&.:;!?$€@№)
АБВГДЕЁЖЗИЙКЛМНОПРСТУФ
ХЦЧШЩЪЫЬЭЮЯабвгдеёжзийкл
мнопрстуфхцчшщъыьэюя

THE QUICK BROWN FOX jumps over a lazy dog. Zwei Boxk mpfer jagen Eva quer durch Sylt. Lorem ipsum dolor sit amet, consectetur adipisicing elit, sed do eiusmod tempor incididunt ut labore et dolore magna aliqua. The quick brown fox jumps over a lazy dog. Zwei Boxk mpfer jagen Eva quer durch Sylt.

Hattori Hanzo – Light Italic	Roman Shamin & Ivan Gladkikh

ABCDEFGHIJKLMNOPQRSTUVWX
YZabcdefghijklmnopqrstuvwxyz
0123456789(&.:;!?$€@№)
АБВГДЕЁЖЗИЙКЛМНОПРСТУФ
ХЦЧШЩЪЫЬЭЮЯабвгдеёжзийкл
мнопрстуфхцчшщъыьэюя

THE QUICK BROWN FOX jumps over a lazy dog. Zwei Boxk mpfer jagen Eva quer durch Sylt. Lorem ipsum dolor sit amet, consectetur adipisicing elit, sed do eiusmod tempor incididunt ut labore et dolore magna aliqua. The quick brown fox jumps over a lazy dog. Zwei Boxk mpfer jagen Eva quer durch Sylt.

London | Olik

QUICK BROWN
JUMPS OVER

ABCDEFGHIJKLMNOPQRSTUVWX
YZ0123456789(!?@)АБВГДЕЁЖЗИ
ЙКЛМНОПРСТУФХЦЧШЩЪЫЬЭЮЯ

Metro | Aleksey Maslov

BROWN

ABCDEFGHIJKLMNOPQR
STUVWXYZABCDEFGHI
JKLMNOPQRSTUVWXY
ZÄÇÉ0123456789(&)АБ
ВГДЕЁЖЗИЙКЛМНОПРС
ТУФХЦЧШЩЪЫЬЭЮЯАБ
ВГДЕЁЖЗИЙКЛМНОПР
СТУФХЦЧШЩЪЫЬЭЮЯ

Molot | Boldhead

BROWN

ABCDEFGHIJKLMNOPQRS
TUVWXYZ0123456789&!?
АБВГДЕЁЖЗИЙКЛМНОПР
СТУФХЦЧШЩЪЫЬЭЮЯ

Neucha | Ivan Gladkikh

Quick brown

ABCDEFGHIJKLMNOPQRSTUVWXY
Zabcdefghijklmnopqrstuvwxyzäçé&
0123456789АБВГДЕЁЖЗИЙКЛМНО
ПРСТУФХЦЧШЩЪЫЬЭЮЯабвгдеё
жзийклмнопрстуфхцчшщъыьэюя

Otscookie	Otscookie

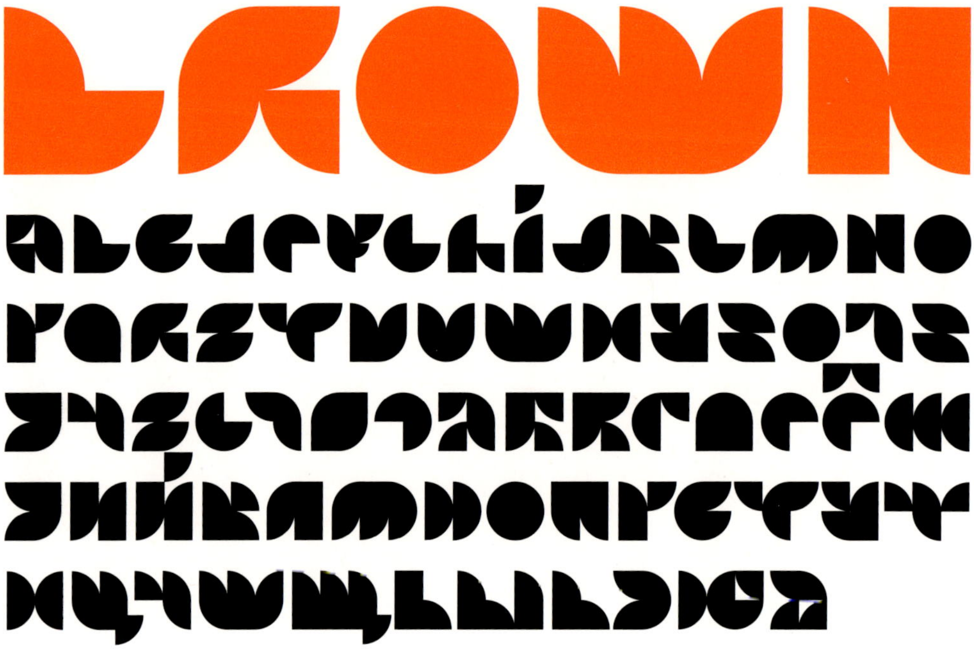

Prosto	Pavel Emelyanov

The quick brown
jumps over a

ABCDEFGHIJKLMNOPQRSTU
VWXYZabcdefghijklmnopqrstu
vwxyząçě0123456789&!?€АБ
ВГДЕЁЖЗИЙКЛМНОПРСТУФ
ХЦЧШЩЪЫЬЭЮЯабвгдеёжзи
йклмнопрстуфхцчшщъыьэюя

Nixie	Ivan Gladkikh

Quick brown

ABCDEFGHIJKLMNOPQRSTU
VWXYZabcdefghijklmnopqrst
uvwxyzäçé0123456789(&:;!?$)

Numans	Ivan Gladkikh

ABCDEFGHIJKLMNOPQRST
UVWXYZabcdefghijklmnop
qrstuvwxyzäçé0123456789

THE QUICK BROWN FOX jumps over a lazy dog. Zwei Boxkämpfer jagen Eva quer durch Sylt. Lorem ipsum dolor sit amet, consectetur adipisicing elit, sed do eiusmod tempor incididunt ut labore et dolore magna

Yeseva	Ivan Gladkikh

Over a lazy

ABCDEFGHIJKLMNOPQRST
UVWXYZabcdefghijklmnop
qrstuvwxyzäçé0123456789

Philosopher – Regular	Ivan Gladkikh

ABCDEFGHIJKLMNOPQRSTUV
WXYZabcdefghijklmnopqrstuvw
xyzäçé0123456789(&:;!?$£€¥№)
АБВГДЕЁЖЗИЙКЛМНОПРСТУ
ФХЦЧШЩЪЫЬЭЮЯабвгдеёжз
ийклмнопрстуфхцчшщъыьэюя

THE QUICK BROWN FOX jumps over a lazy dog. Zwei Boxkämpfer jagen Eva quer durch Sylt. Lorem ipsum dolor sit amet, consectetur adipisicing elit, sed do eiusmod tempor incididunt ut labore et dolore magna aliqua. The quick brown fox jumps over a lazy dog. Zwei Boxkämpfer jagen Eva quer durch Sylt. Lorem ipsum dolor sit amet, consectetur

Philosopher – Italic	Ivan Gladkikh

ABCDEFGHIJKLMNOPQRSTUV
WXYZabcdefghijklmnopqrstuvw
xyzäçé0123456789(&:;!?$€£¥№)
АБВГДЕЁЖЗИЙКЛМНОПРСТУ
ФХЦЧШЩЪЫЬЭЮЯабвгдеёжз
ийклмнопрстуфхцчшщъыьэюя

THE QUICK BROWN FOX jumps over a lazy dog. Zwei Boxkämpfer jagen Eva quer durch Sylt. Lorem ipsum dolor sit amet, consectetur adipisicing elit, sed do eiusmod tempor incididunt ut labore et dolore magna aliqua. The quick brown fox jumps over a lazy dog. Zwei Boxkämpfer jagen Eva quer durch Sylt. Lorem ipsum dolor sit amet, consectetur

Philosopher – Bold	Ivan Gladkikh

ABCDEFGHIJKLMNOPQRSTUV WXYZabcdefghijklmnopqrstuv wxyzäçé0123456789(&:;!?€)АБ ВГДЕЁЖЗИЙКЛМНОПРСТУФ ХЦЧШЩЪЫЬЭЮЯабвгдеёжзи йклмнопрстуфхцчшщъыьэюя

THE QUICK BROWN FOX jumps over a lazy dog. Zwei Boxkämpfer jagen Eva quer durch Sylt. Lorem ipsum dolor sit amet, consectetur adipisicing elit, sed do eiusmod tempor incididunt ut labore et dolore magna aliqua. The quick brown fox jumps over a lazy dog. Zwei Boxkämpfer jagen Eva quer durch Sylt. Lorem ipsum dolor sit amet,

Philosopher – Bold Italic	Ivan Gladkikh

ABCDEFGHIJKLMNOPQRSTUV WXYZabcdefghijklmnopqrstuv wxyzäçé0123456789(&:;!?€)АБ ВГДЕЁЖЗИЙКЛМНОПРСТУФ ХЦЧШЩЪЫЬЭЮЯабвгдеёжзи йклмнопрстуфхцчшщъыьэюя

THE QUICK BROWN FOX jumps over a lazy dog. Zwei Boxkämpfer jagen Eva quer durch Sylt. Lorem ipsum dolor sit amet, consectetur adipisicing elit, sed do eiusmod tempor incididunt ut labore et dolore magna aliqua. The quick brown fox jumps over a lazy dog. Zwei Boxkämpfer jagen Eva quer durch Sylt. Lorem ipsum dolor sit amet,

Jovanny Lemonad | jovanny.ru

Puzzle	Karandashev

BROWN FOX
JUMPS OVER A LAZY
ABCDEFGHIJKLMNOPQRS
TUVWXYZ0123456789C
АБВГДЕЁЖЗИЙКЛМНОП
РСТУФХЦЧШЩЪЫЬЭЮЯ

Russo	Ivan Gladkikh

Fox jumps

ABCDEFGHIJKLMNOPQRSTUV
WXYZabcdefghijklmnopqrstu
vwxyzäçě0123456789(&$€)АБ
ВГДЕЁЖЗИЙКЛМНОПРСТУФХ
ЦЧШЩЪЫЬЭЮЯабвгдеёжзий
клмнопрстуфхцчшщъыьэюя

The quick brown fox jumps OVER a dog

Jovanny Lemonad | jovanny.ru

SuwiKisu	Vonshnauzer

BROWN FOX

ABCDEFGHIJKLMNOPQRSTUVWXYZ

abcdefghijklmnopqrstuvwxyz012345

6789(&:;,.!?$@№❀)АБВГДЕЁЖЗИЙКЛ

МНОПРСТУФХЦЧШЩЪЫЬЭЮЯабвгд

еёжзийклмнопрстуфхцчшщъыьэюя

Zhizn	Peter Zharnov

BROWN FOX

ABCDEFGHIJKLMNOPQRSTUVW

XYZABCDEFGHIJKLMNOPQRSTU

VWXYZ0123456789(&:;!?$€№)

АБВГДЕЁЖЗИЙКЛМНОПРСТУФ

ХЦЧШЩЪЫЬЭЮЯАБВГДЕЁЖЗИЙ

КЛМНОПРСТУФХЦЧШЩЪЫЬЭЮЯ

The League of Moveable Type

theleagueofmoveabletype.com
founders@theleagueofmoveabletype.com

Fanwood – Regular	Barry Schwartz

The quick brown fox jumps

ABCDEFGHIJKLMNOPQRST
UVWXYZabcdefghijklmnopqrstu
vwxyząçě0123456789(&:;!?$£@)
ABCDEFGHIJKLMNOPQRSTUVWXYZ
0123456789

THE QUICK BROWN FOX jumps over a lazy dog. Zwei Boxkämpfer jagen Eva quer durch Sylt. Lorem ipsum dolor sit amet, consectetur adipisicing elit, sed do eiusmod tempor incididunt ut labore et dolore magna aliqua. The quick brown fox jumps over a lazy dog. Zwei Boxkämpfer jagen Eva

Fanwood – Italic	Barry Schwartz

Fox jumps over the

ABCDEFGHIJKLMNOPQRST
UVWXYZabcdefghijklmnopqrstu
vwxyząçě0123456789(&:;!?$£@)
0123456789

THE QUICK BROWN FOX jumps over a lazy dog. Zwei Boxkämpfer jagen Eva quer durch Sylt. Lorem ipsum dolor sit amet, consectetur adipisicing elit, sed do eiusmod tempor incididunt ut labore et dolore magna aliqua. The quick brown fox jumps over a lazy dog. Zwei Boxkämpfer jagen Eva quer durch Sylt. Lorem ipsum dolor sit amet, consectetur adipisicing elit, sed do eiusmod tempor incidid-

Fanwood Text – Regular	Barry Schwartz

The quick brown fox jumps

ABCDEFGHIJKLMNOPQRST
UVWXYZabcdefghijklmnopqrstu
vwxyząçě0123456789(&:;!?$£@)
ABCDEFGHIJKLMNOPQRSTUVWXYZ
0123456789

THE QUICK BROWN FOX jumps over a lazy dog. Zwei Boxkämpfer jagen Eva quer durch Sylt. Lorem ipsum dolor sit amet, consectetur adipisicing elit, sed do eiusmod tempor incididunt ut labore et dolore magna aliqua. The quick brown fox jumps over a lazy dog. Zwei Boxkämpfer jagen Eva

Fanwood Text – Italic	Barry Schwartz

Fox jumps over the

ABCDEFGHIJKLMNOPQRST
UVWXYZabcdefghijklmnopqrstu
vwxyząçě0123456789(&:;!?$£@)
0123456789

THE QUICK BROWN FOX jumps over a lazy dog. Zwei Boxkämpfer jagen Eva quer durch Sylt. Lorem ipsum dolor sit amet, consectetur adipisicing elit, sed do eiusmod tempor incididunt ut labore et dolore magna aliqua. The quick brown fox jumps over a lazy dog. Zwei Boxkämpfer jagen Eva quer durch Sylt. Lorem ipsum dolor sit amet, consectetur adipisicing elit, sed do eiusmod tempor incidid-

Knewave – Regular	Tyler Finck

THE QUICK BROWN

ABCDEFGHIJKLMNOPQRSTUVW
XYZabcdefghijklmnopqrstuvw
xyz0123456789(&:;!?$£€@)

Knewave – Outline	Tyler Finck

THE QUICK BROWN

ABCDEFGHIJKLMNOPQRSTUVW
XYZabcdefghijklmnopqrstuvw
xyz0123456789(&:;!?$£€@)

League Script – Thin	Haley Fiege

Quick brown fox

ABCDEFGHIJKLMNOPQRS
TUVWXYZabcdefghijklmn
opqrstuvwxyzäçé0123456789

Linden Hill – Regular	Barry Schwartz

The quick brown fox jumps

ABCDEFGHIJKLMNOPQRST
UVWXYZabcdefghijklmnopqrstu
vwxyząçě0123456789(&:;!?$£)

ABCDEFGHIJKLMNOPQRSTUVWXYZ
0123456789

THE QUICK BROWN FOX jumps over a lazy dog. Zwei Boxkämpfer jagen Eva quer durch Sylt. Lorem ipsum dolor sit amet, consectetur adipisicing elit, sed do eiusmod tempor incididunt ut labore et dolore magna aliqua. The quick brown fox jumps over a lazy dog. Zwei Boxkämpfer jagen Eva quer

Linden Hill – Italic	Barry Schwartz

The quick brown fox

AABBCCDDEEFGGHIJKLMM
MNNOPPQQRRSTTUVWXYZ
abcdefgghijkklmnopqrstuvwxyzząçě
01234567890123456789(&:;!?$)

THE QUICK BROWN FOX *jumps over a lazy dog. Zwei Boxkämpfer jagen Eva quer durch Sylt. Lorem ipsum dolor sit amet, consectetur adipisicing elit, sed do eiusmod tempor incididunt ut labore et dolore magna aliqua. The quick brown fox jumps over a lazy dog. Zwei Boxkämpfer jagen Eva quer durch Sylt. Lorem ipsum dolor sit amet, consectetur adipisicing elit, sed do eiusmod tempor incididunt ut labore et dolore magna aliqua. The quick brown fox jumps over a*

Ostrich Sans – Condensed Light	Tyler Finck

THE QUICK BROWN FOX
ABCDEFGHIJKLMNOPQRSTU
VWXYZ0123456789(&!?$)

Ostrich Sans – Medium	Tyler Finck

JUMPS OVER A LAZY
ABCDEFGHIJKLMNOPQRSTU
VWXYZ0123456789(&!?$)

Ostrich Sans – Black	Tyler Finck

FOX JUMPS OVER
ABCDEFGHIJKLMNOPQRSTU
VWXYZ0123456789(&!?$)

THE QUICK
BROWN
FOX JUMPS
OVER

Ostrich Sans – Dashed	Tyler Finck

THE QUICK BROWN FOX

ABCDEFGHIJKLMNOPQRSTU
VWXYZ0123456789(&!?$)

Ostrich Sans – Rounded	Tyler Finck

JUMPS OVER A LAZY

ABCDEFGHIJKLMNOPQRSTU
VWXYZ0123456789(&!?$)

Ostrich Sans – Bold	Tyler Finck

FOX JUMPS OVER

ABCDEFGHIJKLMNOPQRSTU
VWXYZ0123456789(&!?$)

Łukasz Dziedzic

latofonts.com
team@latofonts.com

Lato – Hairline | Łukasz Dziedzic

ABCDEFGHIJKLMNOPQRSTU
VWXYZabcdefghijklmnopqrstuv
wxyząçé0123456789(&:;!?$£€)

THE QUICK BROWN FOX jumps over a lazy dog. Zwei Boxkämpfer jagen Eva quer durch Sylt. Lorem ipsum dolor sit amet, consectetur adipisicing elit, sed do eiusmod tempor incididunt ut labore et dolore magna aliqua. The quick brown fox jumps over a lazy dog. Zwei

Lato – Hairline Italic | Łukasz Dziedzic

ABCDEFGHIJKLMNOPQRSTUV
WXYZabcdefghijklmnopqrstuvwxy
ząçé0123456789(&:;!?$¢£¥€@)

THE QUICK BROWN FOX jumps over a lazy dog. Zwei Boxkämpfer jagen Eva quer durch Sylt. Lorem ipsum dolor sit amet, consectetur adipisicing elit, sed do eiusmod tempor incididunt ut labore et dolore magna aliqua. The quick brown fox jumps over a lazy dog. Zwei Boxkämpfer jagen Eva

Lato – Light | Łukasz Dziedzic

ABCDEFGHIJKLMNOPQRSTU
VWXYZabcdefghijklmnopqrstu
vwxyząçé0123456789(&:;!?$€)

THE QUICK BROWN FOX jumps over a lazy dog. Zwei Boxkämpfer jagen Eva quer durch Sylt. Lorem ipsum dolor sit amet, consectetur adipisicing elit, sed do eiusmod tempor incididunt ut labore et dolore magna aliqua. The quick brown fox jumps over a lazy dog. Zwei

The quick
BROWN
fox jumps over
over a lazy
DOG
Zwei Boxkämpfer

Lato – Light Italic	Łukasz Dziedzic

ABCDEFGHIJKLMNOPQRSTUV WXYZabcdefghijklmnopqrstuvwx yząçé0123456789(&:;!?$¢£¥€)

THE QUICK BROWN FOX jumps over a lazy dog. Zwei Boxkämpfer jagen Eva quer durch Sylt. Lorem ipsum dolor sit amet, consectetur adipisicing elit, sed do eiusmod tempor incididunt ut labore et dolore magna aliqua. The quick brown fox jumps over a lazy dog. Zwei Boxkämpfer ja-

Lato – Regular	Łukasz Dziedzic

ABCDEFGHIJKLMNOPQRST UVWXYZabcdefghijklmnopqr stuvwxyząçé0123456789&$!?

THE QUICK BROWN FOX jumps over a lazy dog. Zwei Boxkämpfer jagen Eva quer durch Sylt. Lorem ipsum dolor sit amet, consectetur adipisicing elit, sed do eiusmod tempor incididunt ut labore et dolore magna aliqua. The quick brown fox jumps over a

Lato – Italic	Łukasz Dziedzic

ABCDEFGHIJKLMNOPQRSTUV WXYZabcdefghijklmnopqrstuvw xyząçé0123456789(&:;!?$£¥€)

THE QUICK BROWN FOX jumps over a lazy dog. Zwei Boxkämpfer jagen Eva quer durch Sylt. Lorem ipsum dolor sit amet, consectetur adipisicing elit, sed do eiusmod tempor incididunt ut labore et dolore magna aliqua. The quick brown fox jumps over a lazy dog. Zwei Boxkämpfer

Lato – Bold | Łukasz Dziedzic

ABCDEFGHIJKLMNOPQRST UVWXYZabcdefghijklmnopqr stuvwxyząçé0123456789&!?

THE QUICK BROWN FOX jumps over a lazy dog. Zwei Boxkämpfer jagen Eva quer durch Sylt. Lorem ipsum dolor sit amet, consectetur adipisicing elit, sed do eiusmod tempor incididunt ut labore et dolore magna aliqua. The quick brown fox jumps over

Lato – Bold Italic | Łukasz Dziedzic

ABCDEFGHIJKLMNOPQRSTUV WXYZabcdefghijklmnopqrstuvw xyząçé0123456789(&:;!?$£¥€)

THE QUICK BROWN FOX jumps over a lazy dog. Zwei Boxkämpfer jagen Eva quer durch Sylt. Lorem ipsum dolor sit amet, consectetur adipisicing elit, sed do eiusmod tempor incididunt ut labore et dolore magna aliqua. The quick brown fox jumps over a lazy dog. Zwei

Lato – Black | Łukasz Dziedzic

ABCDEFGHIJKLMNOPQRST UVWXYZabcdefghijklmnopq rstuvwxyząçé0123456789&€

THE QUICK BROWN FOX jumps over a lazy dog. Zwei Boxkämpfer jagen Eva quer durch Sylt. Lorem ipsum dolor sit amet, consectetur adipisicing elit, sed do eiusmod tempor incididunt ut labore et dolore magna aliqua. The quick brown fox jumps

Lato – Black Italic	Łukasz Dziedzic

ABCDEFGHIJKLMNOPQRSTUV WXYZabcdefghijklmnopqrstuv wxyząçé0123456789(&:;!?$€)

THE QUICK BROWN FOX jumps over a lazy dog. Zwei Boxkämpfer jagen Eva quer durch Sylt. Lorem ipsum dolor sit amet, consectetur adipisicing elit, sed do eiusmod tempor incididunt ut labore et dolore magna aliqua. The quick brown fox jumps over a lazy dog. Zwei

Ndiscovered

ndiscovered.com
info@ndiscovered.com

Regular

ABCDEFGHIJKLMNOPQRSTUVWX
YZabcdefghijklmnopqrstuvwxyzą
çě0123456789(&:;!?$¢£¥€@№)
ABCDEFGHIJKLMNOPQRSTUVWXY
Zabcdefghijklmnopqrstuwxyząçě
0123456789
ABCDEFGHIJKLMNOPQRSTUVWXYZ
0123456789

THE QUICK BROWN FOX jumps over a lazy dog. Zwei Boxkämpfer jagen Eva quer durch Sylt. Lorem ipsum dolor sit amet, consectetur adipisicing elit, sed do eiusmod tempor incididunt ut labore et dolore magna aliqua. The quick brown fox jumps over a lazy dog. Zwei Boxkämpfer jagen Eva quer durch Sylt. Lorem ipsum dolor sit amet,

Italic

ABCDEFGHIJKLMNOPQRSTUVWXY
Zabcdefghijklmnopqrstuvwxyząçě
0123456789(&:;!?$¢£¥€@№)

Thin

ABCDEFGHIJKLMNOPQRSTUVWXY
Zabcdefghijklmnopqrstuvwxyząçě
0123456789(&:;!?$¢£¥€@№)

The quick
brown
fox jumps over
A LAZY DOG
Zwei Boxkämpfer
jagen Eva

Thin Italic

ABCDEFGHIJKLMNOPQRSTUVWXY
Zabcdefghijklmnopqrstuvwxyząçě
0123456789(&:;!?$¢£¥€@№)

Extra Light

ABCDEFGHIJKLMNOPQRSTUVWXY
Zabcdefghijklmnopqrstuvwxyząçě
0123456789(&:;!?$¢£¥€@№)

Extra Light Italic

ABCDEFGHIJKLMNOPQRSTUVWXY
Zabcdefghijklmnopqrstuvwxyząçě
0123456789(&:;!?$¢£¥€@№)

Light

ABCDEFGHIJKLMNOPQRSTUVWXY
Zabcdefghijklmnopqrstuvwxyząçě
0123456789(&:;!?$¢£¥€@№)

Light Italic

ABCDEFGHIJKLMNOPQRSTUVWXY
Zabcdefghijklmnopqrstuvwxyząçě
0123456789(&:;!?$¢£¥€@№)

Medium

ABCDEFGHIJKLMNOPQRSTUVWX
YZabcdefghijklmnopqrstuvwxyzą
çě0123456789(&:;!?$¢£¥€@№)

Medium Italic

ABCDEFGHIJKLMNOPQRSTUVWX
YZabcdefghijklmnopqrstuvwxyzą
çě0123456789(&:;!?$¢£¥€@№)

Demi Bold

ABCDEFGHIJKLMNOPQRSTUVWX
YZabcdefghijklmnopqrstuvwxyzą
çě0123456789(&:;!?$¢£¥€@№)

Demi Bold Italic

ABCDEFGHIJKLMNOPQRSTUVWX
YZabcdefghijklmnopqrstuvwxyzą
çě0123456789(&:;!?$¢£¥€@№)

Bold

ABCDEFGHIJKLMNOPQRSTUVWX
YZabcdefghijklmnopqrstuvwxyz
ąçě0123456789(&:;!?$¢£¥€@№)

Bold Italic

ABCDEFGHIJKLMNOPQRSTUVWX
YZabcdefghijklmnopqrstuvwxyzą
çě0123456789(&:;!?$¢£¥€@№)

Extra Bold

ABCDEFGHIJKLMNOPQRSTUVWX
YZabcdefghijklmnopqrstuvwxyz
ąçě0123456789(&:;!?$¢£¥€@№)

Extra Bold Italic

ABCDEFGHIJKLMNOPQRSTUVWX
YZabcdefghijklmnopqrstuvwxyzą
çě0123456789(&:;!?$¢£¥€@№)

Black

ABCDEFGHIJKLMNOPQRSTUVWX
YZabcdefghijklmnopqrstuvwxyz
ąçě0123456789(&:;!?$¢£¥€@№)

Black Italic

ABCDEFGHIJKLMNOPQRSTUVWX
YZabcdefghijklmnopqrstuvwxyz
ąçě0123456789(&:;!?$¢£¥€@№)

The Northern Block

thenorthernblock.co.uk
info@thenorthernblock.co.uk

Aldo – Open	Jonathan Hill

Quick brown

ABCDEFGHIJKLMNOPQRSTUV
WXYZabcdefghijklmnopqrs
tuvwxyzäçé0123456789&?

Bosko – Block	Jonathan Hill

LAZY DOG

ABCDEFGHIJKLMNOPQRST
UVWXYZabcdefghijklmnopq
rstuvwxyzäçé0123456789&!?

Kaine – Block	Jonathan Hill

THE FOX

ABCDEFGHIJKLMNOPQRST
UVWXYZabcdefghijklmnop
qrstuvwxyzäçé0123456789

Kuro – Regular	Jonathan Hill

ABCDEFGHIJKLMNOPQRSTU
VWXYZabcdefghijklmnopqrstuv
wxyząçě0123456789(&:;!?$£€)

THE QUICK BROWN FOX jumps over a lazy dog. Zwei Boxkämpfer jagen Eva quer durch Sylt. Lorem ipsum dolor sit amet, consectetur adipisicing elit, sed do eiusmod tempor incididunt ut labore et dolore magna aliqua. The quick brown fox jumps over

Mekon – Gradient	Jonathan Hill

BROWN FOX

ABCDEFGHIJKLMNOPQRSTU
VWXYZabcdefghijklmnop
qrstuvwxyzäçé0123456789

OricNeo – Stencil	Jonathan Hill

jumps over

ABCDEFGHIJKLMNOPQRSTUV
WXYZabcdefghijklmnopqrst
uvwxyzäçé0123456789(&€)

The Northern Block | thenorthernblock.co.uk

Planer – Regular | Jonathan Hill

ABCDEFGHIJKLMNOPQRSTUV
WXYZabcdefghijklmnopqrstuvw
xyząçě0123456789(&:;!?$£¥€@)

THE QUICK BROWN FOX jumps over a lazy dog. Zwei Boxkämpfer jagen Eva quer durch Sylt. Lorem ipsum dolor sit amet, consectetur adipisicing elit, sed do eiusmod tempor inci-didunt ut labore et dolore magna aliqua. The quick brown fox jumps over a lazy dog. Zwei

Planer – Italic | Jonathan Hill

ABCDEFGHIJKLMNOPQRSTUV
WXYZabcdefghijklmnopqrstuvw
xyząçě0123456789(&:;!?$£¥€@)

THE QUICK BROWN FOX jumps over a lazy dog. Zwei Boxkämpfer jagen Eva quer durch Sylt. Lorem ipsum dolor sit amet, consectetur adipisicing elit, sed do eiusmod tempor inci-didunt ut labore et dolore magna aliqua. The quick brown fox jumps over a lazy dog. Zwei

Scriber – Bold Stencil | Jonathan Hill

Quick brown fox

ABCDEFGHIJKLMNOPQRSTU
VWXYZabcdefghijklmnopqr
stuvwxyzäçé0123456789&

The quick brown fox jumps over A LAZY DOG Zwei Boxkämpfer JAGEN

Sylar – Stencil	Jonathan Hill

Brown fox

ABCDEFGHIJKLMNOPQRSTUV
WXYZabcdefghijklmnopqrs
tuvwxyzäçé0123456789&€

Tondu	Jonathan Hill

The quick fox

ABCDEFGHIJKLMNOPQRSTUV
WXYZabcdefghijklmnopqrstu
vwxyzäçé0123456789&:;!?$€

VanBerger – Stencil	Jonathan Hill

THE QUICK

ABCDEFGHIJKLMNOPQRSTUV
WXYZabcdefghijklmnopqrs
tuvwxyzäçé0123456789&$

Paragraph

paragraph.com.au
paragraph@bigpond.com

Diagond – Light	Jan Schmoeger

Quick brown fox

ABCDEFGHIJKLMNOPQRSTUV
WXYZabcdefghijklmnopqrs
tuvwxyząçě0123456789&!?

Diagond – Bold	Jan Schmoeger

Over a lazy dog

ABCDEFGHIJKLMNOPQRSTUV
WXYZabcdefghijklmnopqr
stuvwxyząçě0123456789$

Tertre – Extra Bold	Jan Schmoeger

The quick brown

ABCDEFGHIJKLMNOPQRSTUV
WXYZabcdefghijklmnopqrstu
vwxyząçě0123456789(&;:!?$€)

Tertre – Extra Bold Italic	Jan Schmoeger

The quick brown

ABCDEFGHIJKLMNOPQRSTUV WXYZabcdefghijklmnopqrstu vwxyząçě0123456789(&;:!?$€)

Springsteel – Light	Jan Schmoeger

ABCDEFGHIJKLMNOPQRSTUVW XYZabcdefghijklmnopqrstuvwxy ząçě0123456789(&:;!?$¢£¥€@)

THE QUICK BROWN FOX jumps over a lazy dog. Zwei Boxkämpfer jagen Eva quer durch Sylt. Lorem ipsum dolor sit amet, consectetur adipisicing elit, sed do eiusmod tempor incididunt ut labore et dolore magna aliqua. The quick brown fox jumps over a lazy dog. Zwei Boxkämpfer

Springsteel – Light Italic	Jan Schmoeger

ABCDEFGHIJKLMNOPQRSTUVW XYZabcdefghijklmnopqrstuvwxy ząçě0123456789(&:;!?$¢£¥€@)

THE QUICK BROWN FOX jumps over a lazy dog. Zwei Boxkämpfer jagen Eva quer durch Sylt. Lorem ipsum dolor sit amet, consectetur adipisicing elit, sed do eiusmod tempor incididunt ut labore et dolore magna aliqua. The quick brown fox jumps over a lazy dog. Zwei Boxkämpfer

Springsteel Serif – Thin | Jan Schmoeger

ABCDEFGHIJKLMNOPQRSTU
VWXYZabcdefghijklmnopqrs
tuvwxyząçě0123456789
ABCDEFGHIJKLMNOPQRSTUVWX
YZ0123456789(&:;!?$¢£¥€@)

THE QUICK BROWN FOX jumps over a lazy dog. Zwei Boxkämpfer jagen Eva quer durch Sylt. Lorem ipsum dolor sit amet, consectetur adipisicing elit, sed do eiusmod tempor incididunt ut labore et dolore magna aliqua. The quick brown fox jumps over a lazy dog. Zwei Boxkämpfer jagen Eva quer durch Sylt. Lorem ipsum dolor sit amet, consectetur adipisicing elit, sed do eiusmod tempor incididunt ut labore et dolore magna aliqua. The

Springsteel Serif – Thin Italic | Jan Schmoeger

ABCDEFGHIJKLMNOPQRSTU
VWXYZabcdefghijklmnopqrs
tuvwxyząçě0123456789
ABCDEFGHIJKLMNOPQRSTUVWX
YZ0123456789(&:;!?$¢£¥€@)

THE QUICK BROWN FOX jumps over a lazy dog. Zwei Boxkämpfer jagen Eva quer durch Sylt. Lorem ipsum dolor sit amet, consectetur adipisicing elit, sed do eiusmod tempor incididunt ut labore et dolore magna aliqua. The quick brown fox jumps over a lazy dog. Zwei Boxkämpfer jagen Eva quer durch Sylt. Lorem ipsum dolor sit amet, consectetur adipisicing elit, sed do eiusmod tempor incididunt ut labore et dolore mag-

The quick brown
FOX JUMPS
over a lazy dog
Zwei Boxkämpfer
jagen Eva
QUER

Springsteel Serif – Heavy | Jan Schmoeger

ABCDEFGHIJKLMNOPQRST
UVWXYZabcdefghijklmnop
qrstuvwxyząçě0123456789
ABCDEFGHIJKLMNOPQRSTUV
WXYZ0123456789(&:;!?$£€)

THE QUICK BROWN FOX jumps over a lazy dog. Zwei Boxkämpfer jagen Eva quer durch Sylt. Lorem ipsum dolor sit amet, consectetur adipisicing elit, sed do eiusmod tempor incididunt ut labore et dolore magna aliqua. The quick brown fox jumps over a lazy dog. Zwei Boxkämpfer jagen Eva quer durch Sylt. Lorem ipsum dolor sit amet, consectetur adipisicing elit, sed do eiusmod tempor incididunt ut

Springsteel Serif – Heavy Italic | Jan Schmoeger

ABCDEFGHIJKLMNOPQRST
UVWXYZabcdefghijklmnop
qrstuvwxyząçě0123456789
ABCDEFGHIJKLMNOPQRSTUV
WXYZ0123456789(&:;!?$£€)

THE QUICK BROWN FOX jumps over a lazy dog. Zwei Boxkämpfer jagen Eva quer durch Sylt. Lorem ipsum dolor sit amet, consectetur adipisicing elit, sed do eiusmod tempor incididunt ut labore et dolore magna aliqua. The quick brown fox jumps over a lazy dog. Zwei Boxkämpfer jagen Eva quer durch Sylt. Lorem ipsum dolor sit amet, consectetur adipisicing elit, sed do eiusmod tempor incididunt ut

Pilcrow Type

pilcrowtype.com
paul@pilcrowtype.com

Med Splode | Paul D. Hunt

THE QUICK
BROWN
FOX JUMPS

ABCDEFGHIJKLMN
OPQRSTUVWXYZa
bcdefghijklmno
pqrstuvwxyz012
3456789(&.:;!?$€@)

SlabStruct | Paul D. Hunt

The brown

ABCDEFGHIJKLMNOPQRSTU
VWXYZabcdefghijklmnopqrs
tuvwxyz0123456789(&.:;!?$¢€@)

SlabStruct Stencil | Paul D. Hunt

The brown

ABCDEFGHIJKLMNOPQRSTU
VWXYZabcdefghijklmnopqrs
tuvwxyz0123456789(&:;!?$¢€@)

SlabStruct Too | Paul D. Hunt

The brown

ABCDEFGHIJKLMNOPQRSTU
VWXYZabcdefghijklmnopqrs
tuvwxyz0123456789(&:;!?@)

SlabStruct Too Soft | Paul D. Hunt

The brown

ABCDEFGHIJKLMNOPQRSTU
VWXYZabcdefghijklmnopqrs
tuvwxyz0123456789(&:;!?@)

Structurosa

Paul D. Hunt

Regular

abcdefghijklmnopqrstuv
wxyząçð0123456789&аб
вгдежзийклмнопрстуф
хцчшщъыьэюяαβγδεζη
θικλμνξοπρσςτυφχψω

Clean

abcdefghijklmnopqrstuv
wxyząçð0123456789&:;!?

Bold

abcdefghijklmnop
qrstuvwxyz&:;!?£
0123456789

Bold Too

abcdefghijklmnop
qrstuvwxyz&:;!?£
0123456789

Caps

ABCDEFGHIJKLMNOPQRSTU
VWXYZabcdefghijklmnop
qrstuvwxyz0123456789

Soft

Brown fox jumps over a
ABCDEFGHIJKLMNOPQRSTU
VWXYZabcdefghijklmnop
qrstuvwxyz0123456789

Clean Soft

Brown fox jumps over a
ABCDEFGHIJKLMNOPQRSTU
VWXYZabcdefghijklmnop
qrstuvwxyz0123456789

Boxy

abcdefghijklmnopqrstuv
wxyzqçð0123456789&!?

Script Clean

The quick brown

ABCDEFGHIJKLMNOPQR
STUVWXYZabcdefghij
klmnopqrstuvwxyz

Script

ABCDEFGHIJKLMNOPQR
STUVWXYZabcdefghij
klmnopqrstuvwxyz

Script Heavy

ABCDEFGHIJKLMN
OPQRSTUVWXYZ
abcdefghijklmno
pqrstuvwxyz

Too

abcdefghijklmnopqrstuv
wxyzãçé0123456789&:;!?

Structurosa Script Clean | Paul D. Hunt

The quick brown fox jumps over a lazy dog Zwel

Pilcrow Type | pilcrowtype.com

Clean Too

abcdefghijklmnopqrstuv
wxyzáçé0123456789&:;!?

Leaf

Brown fox jumps over a
ABCDEFGHIJKLMNOPQRSTU
VWXYZabcdefghijklmnop
qrstuvwxyz0123456789

Clean Leaf

Brown fox jumps over a
ABCDEFGHIJKLMNOPQRSTU
VWXYZabcdefghijklmnop
qrstuvwxyz0123456789

Tape

ABCDEFGHIJKLMNOPQRSTU
VWXYZabcdefghijklmnop
qrstuvwxyz0123456789

Pizzadude

pizzadude.dk
jakob@pizzadude.dk

Asqualt	Jakob Fischer

QUICK BROWN

ABCDEFGHIJKLMNOPQRSTU
VWXYZABCDEFGHIJKLMNOP
QRSTUVWXYZ0123456789&!?

Believe in Me	Jakob Fischer

The quick brown fox jumps over a
fox jumps over a lazy dog

ABCDEFGHIJKLMNOPQRSTUVWXYZabcdef
ghijklmnopqrstuvwxyzãçé0123456789&€

City By the Lake	Jakob Fischer

THE QUICK BROWN

ABCDEFGHIJKLMNOPQRSTUVWXYZABCDEFGHIJ
KLMNOPQRSTUVWXYZÄÇÉ0123456789&:;!?€

Pizzadude | pizzadude.dk

Brutality – Extra | Jakob Fischer

BROWN FOX

ABCDEFGHIJKLMNOPQRST
UVWXYZ0123456789

Brutality – Regular | Jakob Fischer

BROWN FOX

ABCDEFGHIJKLMNOPQRST
UVWXYZ0123456789

Dream Machine | Jakob Fischer

THE QUICK BROWN
FOX JUMPS

ABCDEFGHIJKLMNOPQR
STUVWXYZ0123456789

DT 104	Jakob Fischer

THE QUICK BROWN
FOX JUMPS

ABCDEFGHIJKLMNOPQR
STUVWXYZ0123456789

DT 104 in Outbreak	Jakob Fischer

THE QUICK BROWN
FOX JUMPS

ABCDEFGHIJKLMNOPQR
STUVWXYZ0123456789

Earthquake	Jakob Fischer

QUICK BROWN

ABCDEFGHIJKLMNOPQRSTUVW
XYZ0123456789(:;!?@)

Easily Amused | Jakob Fischer

THE QUICK BROWN FOX JUMPS
JUMPS OVER A LAZY DOG
ABCDEFGHIJKLMNOPQRSTUVWXYZ0123456789

Exit Font (for a Film) | Jakob Fischer

THE QUICK BROWN FOX
JUMPS OVER A
ABCDEFGHIJKLMNOPQRS
TUVWXYZ0123456789&$

Fandango | Jakob Fischer

QUICK BROWN FOX JUMPS
JUMPS OVER A
ABCDEFGHIJKLMNOPQRSTU
VWXYZ0123456789(&:;!?)

FatBoySmiles | Jakob Fischer

FOX DOG

ABCDEFGHIJKLMN
OPQRSTUVWXYZ

Find a Way | Jakob Fischer

BROWN FOX

ABCDEFGHIJKLMN
OPQRSTUVWXYZÄÇ
É0123456789&?£

Find a Way – Worn | Jakob Fischer

BROWN FOX

ABCDEFGHIJKLMN
OPQRSTUVWXYZÄÇ
É0123456789&?£

Funny Farm Hard	Jakob Fischer

JUMPS OVER A LAZY

ABCDEFGHIJKLMNOPQRSTUVWX

YZ0123456789[&:;!?$@]

Funny Farm Soft	Jakob Fischer

JUMPS OVER A LAZY

ABCDEFGHIJKLMNOPQRSTUVWX

YZ0123456789[&:;!?$@]

Gringo Nights	Jakob Fischer

THE QUICK BROWN FOX

ABCDEFGHIJKLMNOPQRSTUVWXY

Z0123456789(&:;!?$@)

John Doe	Jakob Fischer

The brown

ABCDEFGHIJKLMNOPQRSTUVWX
YZabcdefghijklmnopqrs
tuvwxyz0123456789(:;!?$@)

Knuckle Sandwich	Jakob Fischer

THE QUICK BROWN
FOX JUMPS

ABCDEFGHIJKLMNOPQRS
TUVWXYZ0123456789(&:;!?)

Make Things Right	Jakob Fischer

The quick brown fox jumps over
jumps over a lazy dog

ABCDEFGHIJKLMNOPQRSTUVWXYZabcdefghijklm
nopqrstuvwxyzäçé0123456789(&:;!?$¢£¥€)

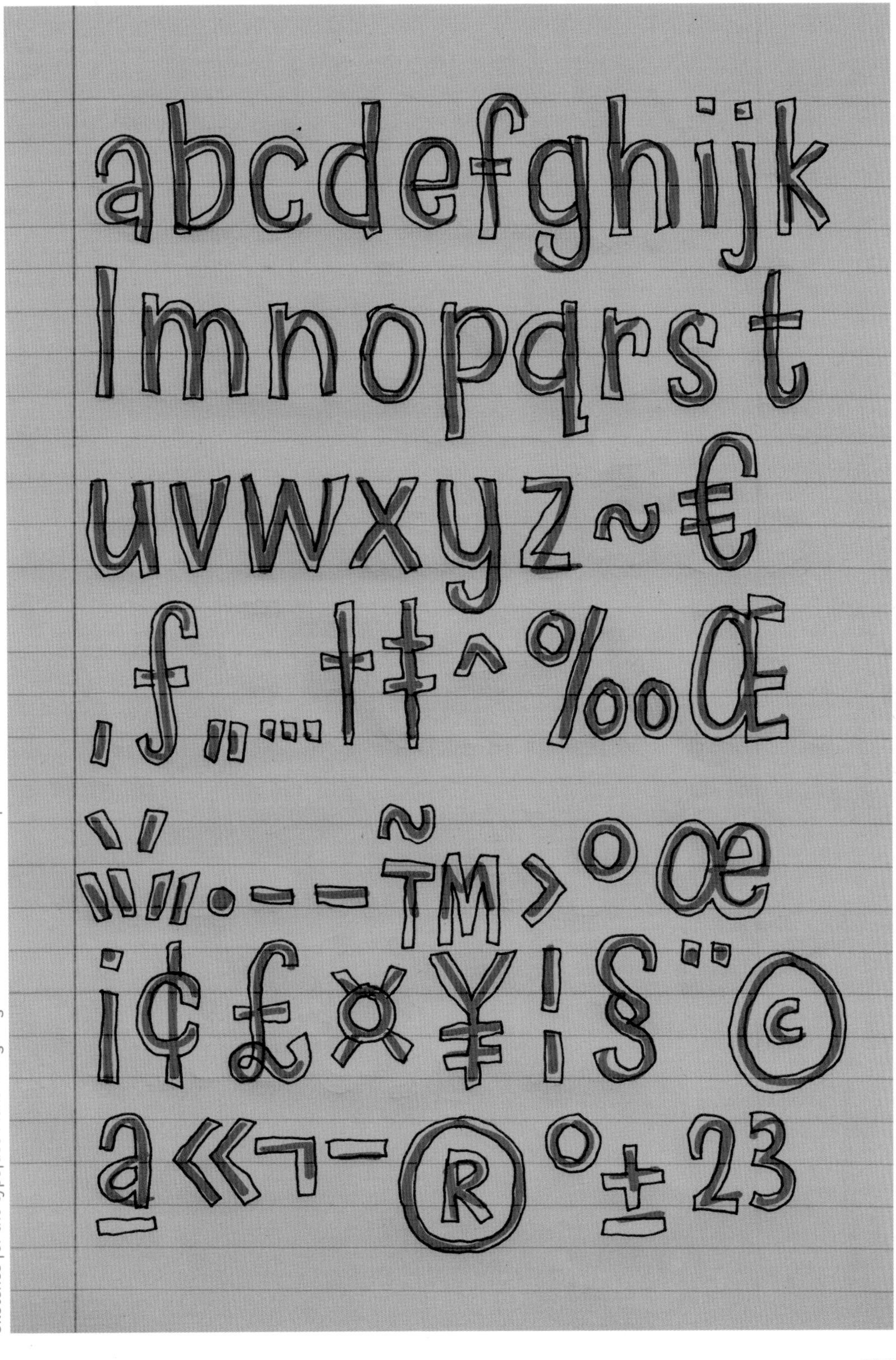

Sketches for the typeface Make Things Right. © 2012 Jakob Fischer | Pizzadude

Kookaburra | Jakob Fischer

The quick brown

ABCDEFGHIJKLMNOPQRS
TUVWXYZabcdefghijklmnopqr
stuvwxyz0123456789(&:;!?$@)

Krazy Nights | Jakob Fischer

QUICK BROWN
LAZY DOG

ABCDEFGHIJKLMNOP
QRSTUVWXYZ(&!?$@)

Marmelade Guys | Jakob Fischer

quick fox

abcdefghijklmn
opqrstuvwxyz
0123456789<:;!?$@>

Miserable	Jakob Fischer

THE QUICK BROWN FOX JUMPS OVER A LAZY DOG

ABCDEFGHIJKLMNOPQRSTUVWXYZ0123456789

MuchoMacho	Jakob Fischer

THE QUICK BROWN FOX JUMPS

ABCDEFGHIJKLMNOPQRST
UVWXYZ0123456789&:;!?

Not a Chance	Jakob Fischer

The quick brown fox

ABCDEFGHIJKLMNOPQRSTUVWXYZ
abcdefghijklmnopqrstuvwxyz
äçé0123456789(&:;!?$¢£¥€@)

Not Just a Toy | Jakob Fischer

QUICK BROWN
FOX JUMPS

ABCDEFGHIJKLMNOPQR
STUVWXYZ0123456789

Oxygene | Jakob Fischer

THE QUICK BROWN FOX JUMPS
OVER A LAZY DOG

ABCDEFGHIJKLMNOPQRSTUVWXY
Z0123456789(&:;!?$)

Piece of Youth | Jakob Fischer

THE QUICK BROWN FOX JUMPS
BROWN FOX JUMPS OVER A LAZY DOG

ABCDEFGHIJKLMNOPQRSTUVWXYZABCDEFGH
IJKLMNOPQRSTUVWXYZÄÇÉ0123456789&!?€

Permanent Daylight – Regular	Jakob Fischer

THE QUICK BROWN FOX

ABCDEFGHIJKLMNOPQRSTUVWXYZabcdefghij
klmnopqrstuvwxyzäàcé0123456789(&:;!?)

Permanent Daylight – Italic	Jakob Fischer

THE QUICK BROWN FOX

ABCDEFGHIJKLMNOPQRSTUVWXYZabcdefghij
klmnopqrstuvwxyzäàcé0123456789(&:;!?)

Piracy	Jakob Fischer

A QUICK BROWN FOX
JUMPS OVER

ABCDEFGHIJKLMNOPQ
RSTUVWXYZ0123456789

PizzaBot	Jakob Fischer

the brown

abcdefghijklmnop
qrstuvwxyzäçé
0123456789(:;!?$@)

Poft Sarade	Jakob Fischer

THE FOX

ABCDEFGHIJKLMNOPQRSTU
VWXYZABCDEFGHIJKLMNOP
QRSTUVWXYZ0123456789?

Raveheart	Jakob Fischer

THE QUICK BROWN

ABCDEFGHIJKLMNOPQR
STUVWXYZABCDEFGHIJ
KLMNOPQRSTUVWXYZÄÇ
$0123456789(&:;!?)

Sk8 or Dye	Jakob Fischer

BROWN FOX JUMPS

ABCDEFGHIJKLMNOPQRSTUVWX
YZABCDEFGHIJKLMNOPQRSTUVW
XYZ0123456789(&.:;!?$@)

Strange Phenomena – Normal	Jakob Fischer

BROWN FOX

ABCDEFGHIJKLMNOPQRS
TUVWXYZ0123456789(!?)

Streetwise Buddy	Jakob Fischer

LAZY DOG

ABCDEFGHIJKLMNOPQRSTU
VWXYZABCDEFGHIJKLMNOP
QRSTUVWXYZÄÇÉ0123456789

TagsXtreme	Jakob Fischer

DOG FOX

ABCDEFGHIJKLMNO
PQRSTUVWXYZ

Up to the Light	Jakob Fischer

QUICK BROWN

ABCDEFGHIJKLMNOPQRSTUVWX
YZÄÇÉ0123456789(&:;!?$£€@)

Urgency of Now	Jakob Fischer

THE QUICK FOX

ABCDEFGHIJKLMNOPQRSTUVWXYZabcdefghij
klmnopqrstuvwxyzäçé0123456789&!?$£¥€

Videophreak | Jakob Fischer

Brown fox

ABCDEFGHIJKLMNOPQRST
UVWXYZabcdefghijklmnop
qrstuvwxyz0123456789@?

You Could Be Right | Jakob Fischer

Fox jumps over a lazy dog

ABCDEFGHIJKLMNOPQRSTUVW
XYZabcdefghijklmnopqrstuvwx
yzäçé0123456789(&:;!?$£¥€@)

Youthquake | Jakob Fischer

The brown fox

ABCDEFGHIJKLMNOPQRST
UVWXYZabcdefghijklmnopq
rstuvwxyz0123456789(:;!?$@)

Zipper Blues – Black	Jakob Fischer

THE DOG

ABCDEFGHIJKLMNOPQR
STUVWXYZ0123456789

Zipper Blues – Outline	Jakob Fischer

THE DOG

ABCDEFGHIJKLMNOPQR
STUVWXYZ0123456789

Zitcream	Jakob Fischer

Quick brown fox jumps

ABCDEFGHIJKLMNOPQRSTU
VWXYZabcdefghijklmnopqrstuvw
xyz0123456789(&:;!?$@)

Shamfonts

shamfonts.com
shamfonts@shamrocking.com

Fair – Regular	Shamrock

Lazy dog

ABCDEFGHIJKLMNOPQRSTU
VWXYZabcdefghijklmnopqrs
tuvwxyzäçé0123456789&!?€

Shample 02	Shamrock

Quick brown fox

ABCDEFGHIJKLMNOPQRSTUVWXYZabcde
fghijklmnopqrstuvwxyz0123456789!?

Shamporter	Shamrock

Jumps over

ABCDEFGHIJKLMNOPQRSTUV
WXYZabcdefghijklmnopqr
stuvwxyzäçé0123456789&

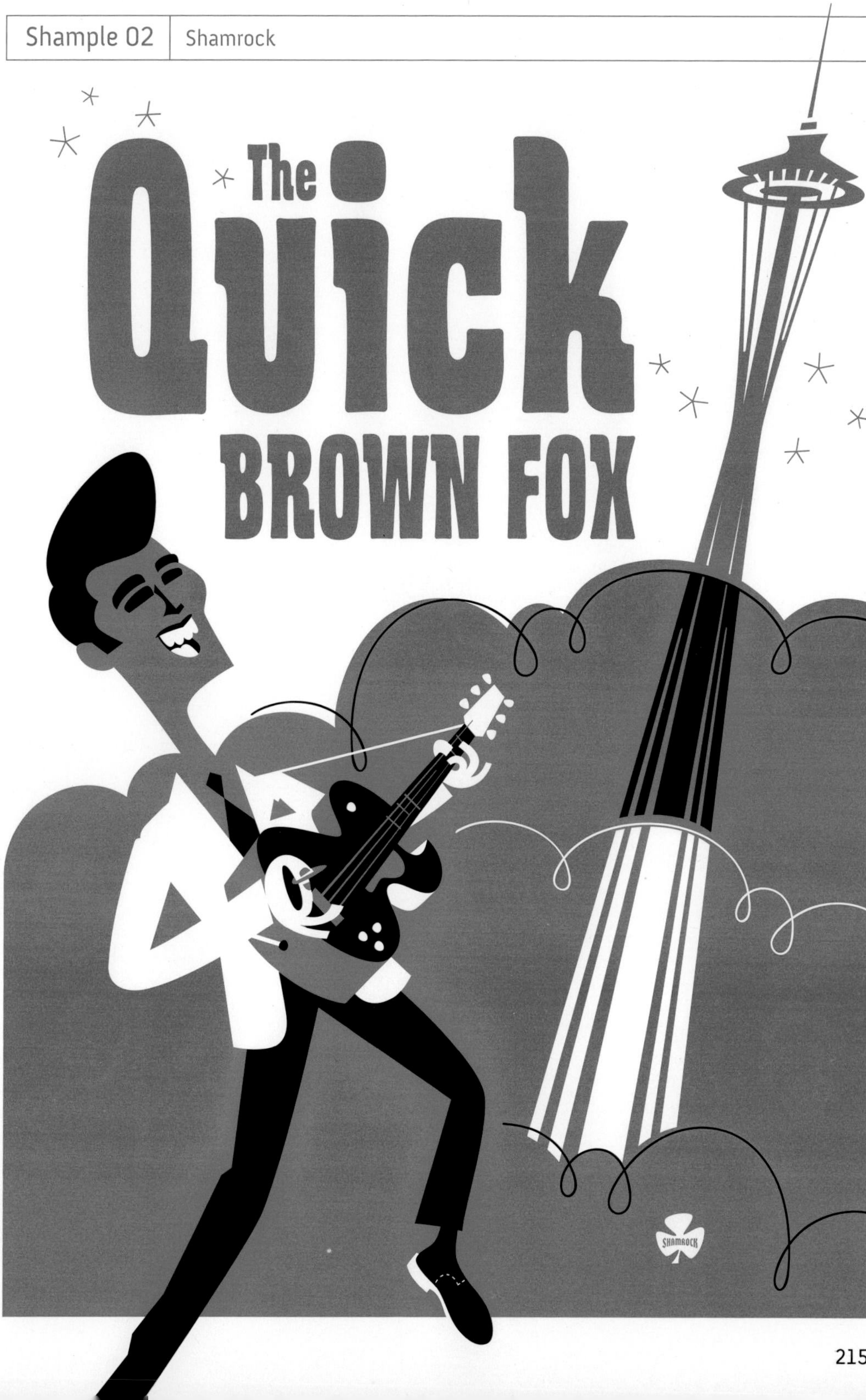
The
Quick
BROWN FOX
SHAMROCK

Shamools 2 | Shamrock

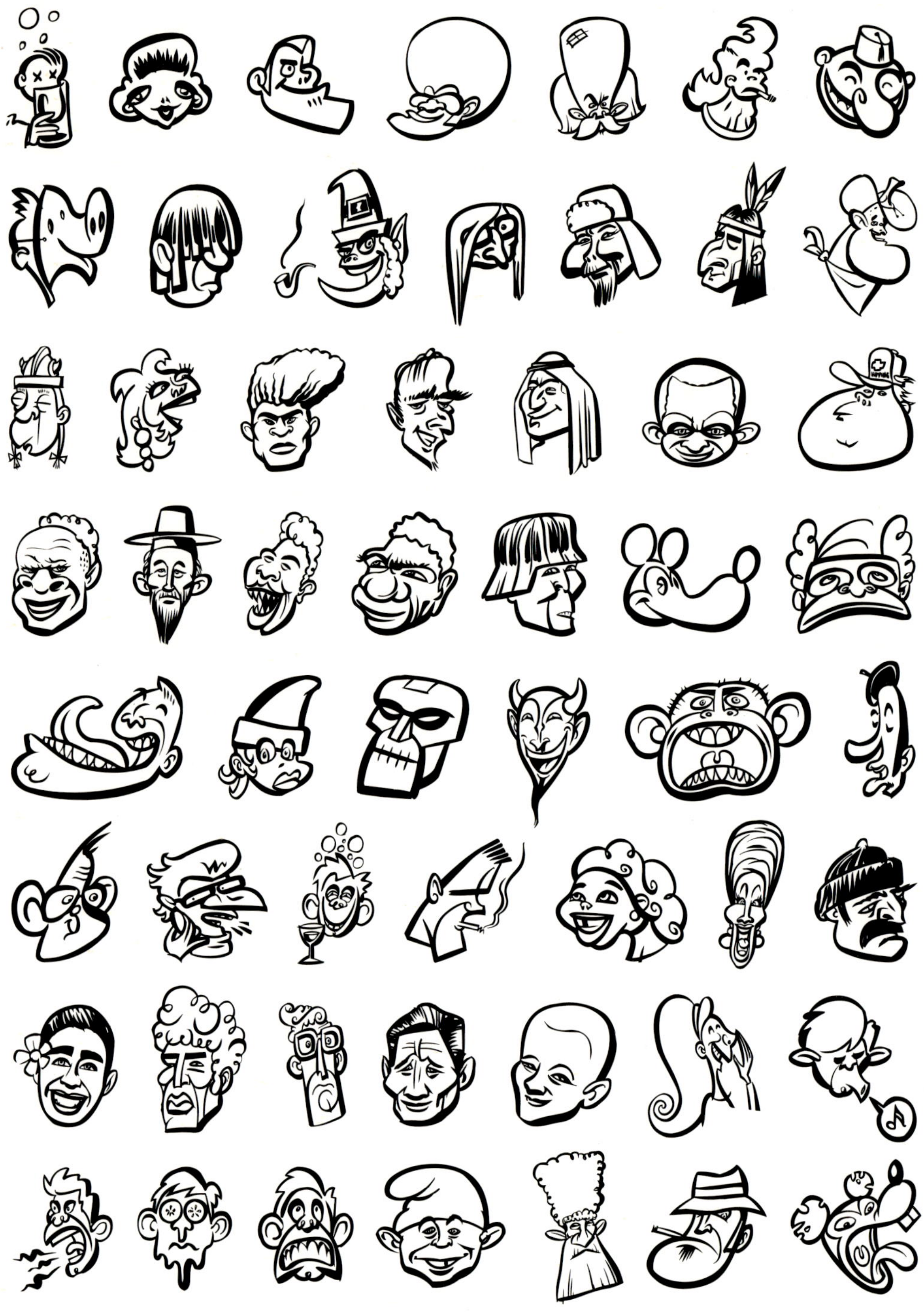

Synthview

typography.synthview.com
typography@synthview.com

Novecento Wide – Light	Jan Tonellato

A FOX JUMPS

ABCDEFGHIIJJKLMNNOPQ
QRSTUVWXYY¥ZĄÇĚ012345
6789(&:;!?$¢£¥€@№)

Novecento Wide – Book	Jan Tonellato

A FOX JUMPS

ABCDEFGHIIJJKLMNNOPQ
QRSTUVWXYY¥ZĄÇĚ012345
6789(&:;!?$¢£¥€@№)

Novecento Wide – Normal	Jan Tonellato

A FOX JUMPS

ABCDEFGHIIJJKLMNNOP
QQRSTUVWXYY¥ZĄÇĚ0123
456789(&:;!?$¢£¥€@№)

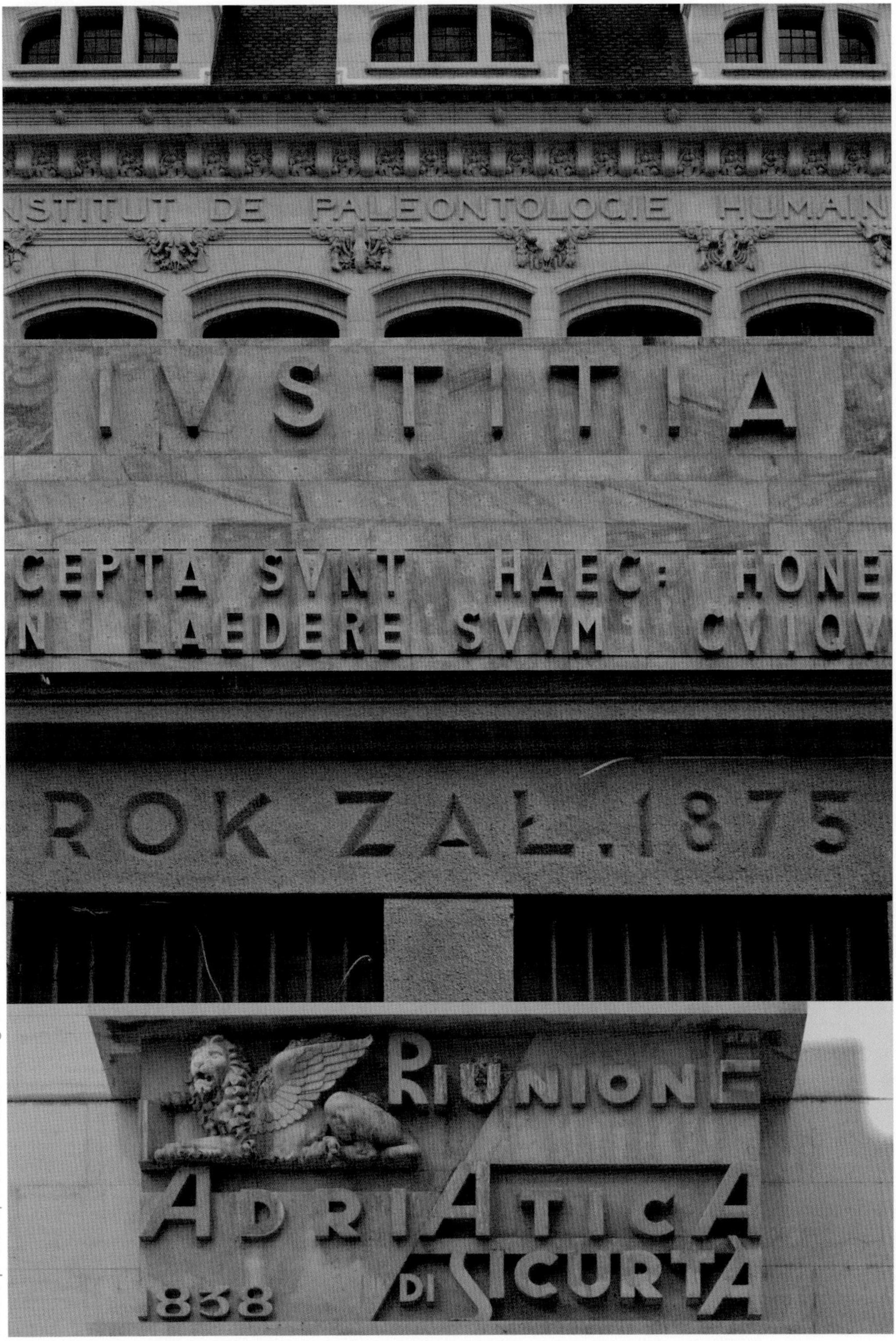

Several photos of architectural lettering that were the inspiration for the typeface Novecento.

Novecento Wide – Medium	Jan Tonellato

JUMPS OVER
ABCDEFGHIIJJKLMNNOP
QQRSTUVWXYY¥ZĄÇĚ0123
456789(&:;!?$¢£¥€@№)

Novecento Wide – Demi Bold	Jan Tonellato

JUMPS OVER
ABCDEFGHIIJJKLMNNOP
QQRSTUVWXYY¥ZĄÇĚ0123
456789(&:;!?$¢£¥€@№)

Novecento Wide – Bold	Jan Tonellato

JUMPS OVER
ABCDEFGHIIJJKLMNNOP
QQRSTUVWXYY¥ZĄÇĚ012
3456789(&:;!?$¢£¥€@№)

Typedifferent

typedifferent.com
typedifferent@burodestruct.net

BD Baldrian	Büro Destruct

BROWN FOX JUMPS

ABCDEFGHIJKLMNOPQRST
UUVWXYZÄÇÉ0123456789(!?)

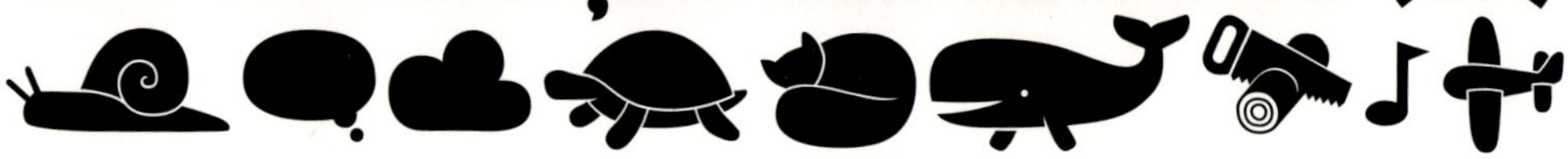

BD Circo	Büro Destruct

The quick brown

ABCDEFGHIJKLMNOPQRST
UVWXYZabcdefghijklmnop
qrstuvwxyz0123456789(&!?)

BD Halfpipe	Büro Destruct

JUMPS OVER

ABCDEFGHIJKLMN
OPQRSTUVWXYZÄÇ
É0123456789(!?

BD Mustang	Büro Destruct

A lazy dog

ABCDEFGHIJKLMNOPQRSTUVWXYZabcdef
ghijklmnopqrstuvwxyzäçé0123456789

BD Pipe	Büro Destruct

Brown Fox

ABCDEFGHIJKLMNOPQRSTUV
WXYZabcdefghijklmnopqrst
uvwxyzäçé0123456789&:;!?/

BD Plankton	Büro Destruct

QUICK BROWN

ABCDEFGHIJKLMNOPQRSTUVW
XYZabcdefghijklmnopqrstuvw
xyząčé0123456789(&:;!?$£¥€@)

BD Ragout	Büro Destruct

Jumps over a lazy

ABCDEFGHIJKLMNOPQRSTUVWXYZ
abcdefghijklmnopqrstuvwxyząçě
0123456789[&:;!?$¢£¥€@]

BD Reithalle	Büro Destruct

THE QUICK FOX
JUMPS OVER

ABCDEFGHIJKLMNOPQRSTUV
WXYZABCDEFGHIJKLMNOPQR
STUVWXYZĄÇĚ0123456789

BD Solaris	Büro Destruct

the quick brown
fox jumps over

abcdefghijklmnopqrs
tuvwxyzäçé0123456789

the quick
brown
fox jumps over
a lazy dog
zwei
boxkämpfer

BD Relaunch	Büro Destruct

THE DOG

ABCDEFGHIJKLMNOPQR
STUVWXYZ 0123456789

BD Times New Digital – Regular	Büro Destruct

FOX JUMPS

ABCDEFGHIJKLMNOPQRSTU
VWXYZabcdefghijklmnopqrstu
vwxyząçé0123456789(&:;?$¢£¥€)

BD Times New Digital – Bold	Büro Destruct

FOX JUMPS

ABCDEFGHIJKLMNOPQRSTU
VWXYZabcdefghijklmnopqrstu
vwxyząçé0123456789(&:;?$¢£¥€)

BD Times New Digital Stencil – Regular | Büro Destruct

FOX JUMPS

ABCDEFGHIJKLMNOPQRSTU
VWXYZabcdefghijklmnopqrstu
vwxyząçé0123456789(&:;?$¢£¥€)

BD Times New Digital Stencil – Bold | Büro Destruct

FOX JUMPS

ABCDEFGHIJKLMNOPQRSTU
VWXYZabcdefghijklmnopqrstu
vwxyząçé0123456789(&:;?$¢£¥€)

BD Times New Digital Bad | Büro Destruct

FOX JUMPS

ABCDEFGHIJKLMNOPQRSTU
VWXYZabcdefghijklmnopqrstu
vwxyząçé0123456789(&:;?$¢£¥€)

BD SpicyFruits – Brush | Büro Destruct

BROWN FOX

ABCDEFGHIJKLMNOPQRSTUV
WXYZabcdefghijklmnopqr
stuvwxyz0123456789&:;!?@

BD SpicyFruits – Regular | Büro Destruct

BROWN FOX

ABCDEFGHIJKLMNOPQRSTUV
WXYZabcdefghijklmnopqr
stuvwxyz0123456789&:;!?@

BD Stella | Büro Destruct

JUMPS OVER A LAZY

ABCDEFGHIJKLMNOPQRSTUVWXYZabcdefgh
ijklmnopqrstuvwxyz0123456789(&:;!?$€@)

Typemade

typemade.mx
hi@typemade.mx

Antic | Santiago Orozco

ABCDEFGHIJKLMNOPQRSTUV WXYZabcdefghijklmnopqrstuv wxyzäçé0123456789(&!?$€)

THE QUICK BROWN FOX jumps over a lazy dog. Zwei Boxkämpfer jagen Eva quer durch Sylt. Lorem ipsum dolor sit amet, consectetur adipisicing elit, sed do eiusmod tempor incididunt ut labore et dolore magna aliqua. The quick brown fox jumps over a lazy dog. Zwei

Antic Didone | Santiago Orozco

ABCDEFGHIJKLMNOPQRSTUV WXYZabcdefghijklmnopqrst uvwxyzäçé0123456789(&!?)

THE QUICK BROWN FOX jumps over a lazy dog. Zwei Boxkämpfer jagen Eva quer durch Sylt. Lorem ipsum dolor sit amet, consectetur adipisicing elit, sed do eiusmod tempor incididunt ut labore et dolore magna aliqua. The quick brown fox jumps over

Antic Slab | Santiago Orozco

ABCDEFGHIJKLMNOPQRSTU VWXYZabcdefghijklmnopqr stuvwxyzäçé0123456789&€

THE QUICK BROWN FOX jumps over a lazy dog. Zwei Boxkämpfer jagen Eva quer durch Sylt. Lorem ipsum dolor sit amet, consectetur adipisicing elit, sed do eiusmod tempor incididunt ut labore et dolore magna aliqua. The quick brown fox jumps over

The quick
brown
fox jumps over
a lazy dog
ZWEI

Dorsa	Santiago Orozco

The quick brown fox jumps over a lazy dog

ABCDEFGHIJKLMNOPQRSTUVWXYZabcdefghijklmnop

qrstuvwxyzäçé0123456789(&:;!?$¢£¥€@)

Josefin Sans – Thin	Santiago Orozco

ABCDEFGHIJKLMNOPQRSTUV

WXYZabcdefghijklmnopqrstuvw

xyzäçé0123456789(&:;!?$¢£¥@)

THE QUICK BROWN FOX jumps over a lazy dog. Zwei Boxkämpfer jagen Eva quer durch Sylt. Lorem ipsum dolor sit amet, consectetur adipisicing elit, sed do eiusmod tempor incididunt ut labore et dolore magna aliqua. The quick brown fox jumps over a lazy dog. Zwei Boxkämp-

Josefin Sans – Thin Italic	Santiago Orozco

ABCDEFGHIJKLMNOPQRSTU

VWXYZabcdefghijklmnopqrstuv

wxyzäçé0123456789(&:;!?$£¥@)

THE QUICK BROWN FOX jumps over a lazy dog. Zwei Boxkämpfer jagen Eva quer durch Sylt. Lorem ipsum dolor sit amet, consectetur adipisicing elit, sed do eiusmod tempor incididunt ut labore et dolore magna aliqua. The quick brown fox jumps over a lazy dog. Zwei Boxkämp-

Josefin Sans – Light | Santiago Orozco

ABCDEFGHIJKLMNOPQRSTUV
WXYZabcdefghijklmnopqrstuvw
xyzäçé0123456789(&:;!?$¢£¥@)

THE QUICK BROWN FOX jumps over a lazy dog. Zwei Boxkämpfer jagen Eva quer durch Sylt. Lorem ipsum dolor sit amet, consectetur adipisicing elit, sed do eiusmod tempor incididunt ut labore et dolore magna aliqua. The quick brown fox jumps over a lazy dog. Zwei Boxkämp-

Josefin Sans – Light Italic | Santiago Orozco

ABCDEFGHIJKLMNOPQRSTU
VWXYZabcdefghijklmnopqrstuv
wxyzäçé0123456789(&:;!?$£¥@)

THE QUICK BROWN FOX jumps over a lazy dog. Zwei Boxkämpfer jagen Eva quer durch Sylt. Lorem ipsum dolor sit amet, consectetur adipisicing elit, sed do eiusmod tempor incididunt ut labore et dolore magna aliqua. The quick brown fox jumps over a lazy dog. Zwei Boxkämp-

Josefin Sans – Regular | Santiago Orozco

ABCDEFGHIJKLMNOPQRSTU
VWXYZabcdefghijklmnopqrstuv
wxyzäçé0123456789(&:;!?$¢£¥)

THE QUICK BROWN FOX jumps over a lazy dog. Zwei Boxkämpfer jagen Eva quer durch Sylt. Lorem ipsum dolor sit amet, consectetur adipisicing elit, sed do eiusmod tempor incididunt ut labore et dolore magna aliqua. The quick brown fox jumps over a lazy dog. Zwei Boxkämp-

Josefin Sans – Italic | Santiago Orozco

ABCDEFGHIJKLMNOPQRSTU VWXYZabcdefghijklmnopqrstuv wxyzäçé0123456789(&:;!?$¢£¥)

THE QUICK BROWN FOX jumps over a lazy dog. Zwei Boxkämpfer jagen Eva quer durch Sylt. Lorem ipsum dolor sit amet, consectetur adipisicing elit, sed do eiusmod tempor incididunt ut labore et dolore magna aliqua. The quick brown fox jumps over a lazy dog. Zwei Boxkämp-

Josefin Sans – Semibold | Santiago Orozco

ABCDEFGHIJKLMNOPQRSTU VWXYZabcdefghijklmnopqrstuv wxyzäçé0123456789(&:;!?$¢£¥)

THE QUICK BROWN FOX jumps over a lazy dog. Zwei Boxkämpfer jagen Eva quer durch Sylt. Lorem ipsum dolor sit amet, consectetur adipisicing elit, sed do eiusmod tempor incididunt ut labore et dolore magna aliqua. The quick brown fox jumps over a lazy dog. Zwei Boxkämp-

Josefin Sans – Semibold Italic | Santiago Orozco

ABCDEFGHIJKLMNOPQRSTU VWXYZabcdefghijklmnopqrstuv wxyzäçé0123456789(&:;!?$¢£¥)

THE QUICK BROWN FOX jumps over a lazy dog. Zwei Boxkämpfer jagen Eva quer durch Sylt. Lorem ipsum dolor sit amet, consectetur adipisicing elit, sed do eiusmod tempor incididunt ut labore et dolore magna aliqua. The quick brown fox jumps over a lazy dog. Zwei Boxkämp-

Josefin Sans – Bold	Santiago Orozco

ABCDEFGHIJKLMNOPQRSTU
VWXYZabcdefghijklmnopqrstuv
wxyzäçé0123456789(&:;!?$¢£¥)

THE QUICK BROWN FOX jumps over a lazy dog. Zwei Boxkämpfer jagen Eva quer durch Sylt. Lorem ipsum dolor sit amet, consectetur adipisicing elit, sed do eiusmod tempor incid-idunt ut labore et dolore magna aliqua. The quick brown fox jumps over a lazy dog. Zwei

Josefin Sans – Bold Italic	Santiago Orozco

ABCDEFGHIJKLMNOPQRSTU
VWXYZabcdefghijklmnopqrstuv
wxyzäçé0123456789(&:;!?$¢£¥)

THE QUICK BROWN FOX jumps over a lazy dog. Zwei Boxkämpfer jagen Eva quer durch Sylt. Lorem ipsum dolor sit amet, consectetur adipisicing elit, sed do eiusmod tempor incid-idunt ut labore et dolore magna aliqua. The quick brown fox jumps over a lazy dog. Zwei

Josefin Slab – Thin	Santiago Orozco

ABCDEFGHIJKLMNOPQRSTU
VWXYZabcdefghijklmnopqrstu
vwxyzäçé0123456789(&:;!?$£¥)

THE QUICK BROWN FOX jumps over a lazy dog. Zwei Boxkämpfer jagen Eva quer durch Sylt. Lorem ipsum dolor sit amet, consectetur adipisicing elit, sed do eiusmod tempor in-cididunt ut labore et dolore magna aliqua. The quick brown fox jumps over a lazy dog. Zwei

Josefin Slab – Thin Italic | Santiago Orozco

ABCDEFGHIJKLMNOPQRSTU
VWXYZabcdefghijklmnopqrstu
vwxyzäçé0123456789(&:;!?$£¥)

THE QUICK BROWN FOX jumps over a lazy dog. Zwei Boxkämpfer jagen Eva quer durch Sylt. Lorem ipsum dolor sit amet, consectetur adipisicing elit, sed do eiusmod tempor incididunt ut labore et dolore magna aliqua. The quick brown fox jumps over a lazy dog. Zwei

Josefin Slab – Light | Santiago Orozco

ABCDEFGHIJKLMNOPQRSTU
VWXYZabcdefghijklmnopqrstu
vwxyzäçé0123456789(&:;!?$£¥)

THE QUICK BROWN FOX jumps over a lazy dog. Zwei Boxkämpfer jagen Eva quer durch Sylt. Lorem ipsum dolor sit amet, consectetur adipisicing elit, sed do eiusmod tempor incididunt ut labore et dolore magna aliqua. The quick brown fox jumps over a lazy dog.

Josefin Slab – Light Italic | Santiago Orozco

ABCDEFGHIJKLMNOPQRSTU
VWXYZabcdefghijklmnopqrstu
vwxyzäçé0123456789(&:;!?$£¥)

THE QUICK BROWN FOX jumps over a lazy dog. Zwei Boxkämpfer jagen Eva quer durch Sylt. Lorem ipsum dolor sit amet, consectetur adipisicing elit, sed do eiusmod tempor incididunt ut labore et dolore magna aliqua. The quick brown fox jumps over a lazy dog.

Josefin Slab – Regular | Santiago Orozco

ABCDEFGHIJKLMNOPQRSTU
VWXYZabcdefghijklmnopqrstu
vwxyzäçé0123456789(&:;!?$£¥)

THE QUICK BROWN FOX jumps over a lazy dog. Zwei Boxkämpfer jagen Eva quer durch Sylt. Lorem ipsum dolor sit amet, consectetur adipisicing elit, sed do eiusmod tempor incididunt ut labore et dolore magna aliqua. The quick brown fox jumps over a lazy dog.

Josefin Slab – Italic | Santiago Orozco

ABCDEFGHIJKLMNOPQRSTU
VWXYZabcdefghijklmnopqrstu
vwxyzäçé0123456789(&:;!?$£¥)

THE QUICK BROWN FOX jumps over a lazy dog. Zwei Boxkämpfer jagen Eva quer durch Sylt. Lorem ipsum dolor sit amet, consectetur adipisicing elit, sed do eiusmod tempor incididunt ut labore et dolore magna aliqua. The quick brown fox jumps over a lazy dog.

Josefin Slab – Semibold | Santiago Orozco

ABCDEFGHIJKLMNOPQRSTU
VWXYZabcdefghijklmnopqrst
uvwxyzäçé0123456789&:;!?$£¥

THE QUICK BROWN FOX jumps over a lazy dog. Zwei Boxkämpfer jagen Eva quer durch Sylt. Lorem ipsum dolor sit amet, consectetur adipisicing elit, sed do eiusmod tempor incididunt ut labore et dolore magna aliqua. The quick brown fox jumps over a lazy

Josefin Slab – Semibold Italic | Santiago Orozco

ABCDEFGHIJKLMNOPQRSTU VWXYZabcdefghijklmnopqrstu vwxyzäçé0123456789(&:;!?$£¥)

THE QUICK BROWN FOX jumps over a lazy dog. Zwei Boxkämpfer jagen Eva quer durch Sylt. Lorem ipsum dolor sit amet, consectetur adipisicing elit, sed do eiusmod tempor incididunt ut labore et dolore magna aliqua. The quick brown fox jumps over a lazy

Josefin Slab – Bold | Santiago Orozco

ABCDEFGHIJKLMNOPQRSTU VWXYZabcdefghijklmnopqrst uvwxyzäçé0123456789&:;!?$£¥

THE QUICK BROWN FOX jumps over a lazy dog. Zwei Boxkämpfer jagen Eva quer durch Sylt. Lorem ipsum dolor sit amet, consectetur adipisicing elit, sed do eiusmod tempor incididunt ut labore et dolore magna aliqua. The quick brown fox jumps over a lazy

Josefin Slab – Bold Italic | Santiago Orozco

ABCDEFGHIJKLMNOPQRSTU VWXYZabcdefghijklmnopqrst uvwxyzäçé0123456789&:;!?$£¥

THE QUICK BROWN FOX jumps over a lazy dog. Zwei Boxkämpfer jagen Eva quer durch Sylt. Lorem ipsum dolor sit amet, consectetur adipisicing elit, sed do eiusmod tempor incididunt ut labore et dolore magna aliqua. The quick brown fox jumps over a lazy

TypeType

typetype.net
info@typetype.net

Blockit – Thin | Dirk Uhlenbrock

The dog

AaBbCDdEEeFGgHhIIJ
KLLMNOPQRrSTtUVWX
YyZ0123456789[G$]

Blockit – Normal | Dirk Uhlenbrock

The dog

AaBbCDdEEeFGgHhIIJ
KLLMNOPQRrSTtUVWX
YyZ0123456789[G$]

Blockit – Bold | Dirk Uhlenbrock

The dog

AaBbCDdEEeFGgHhIIJ
KLLMNOPQRrSTtUVWX
YyZ0123456789[G$]

Buddies (selection)	Dirk Uhlenbrock

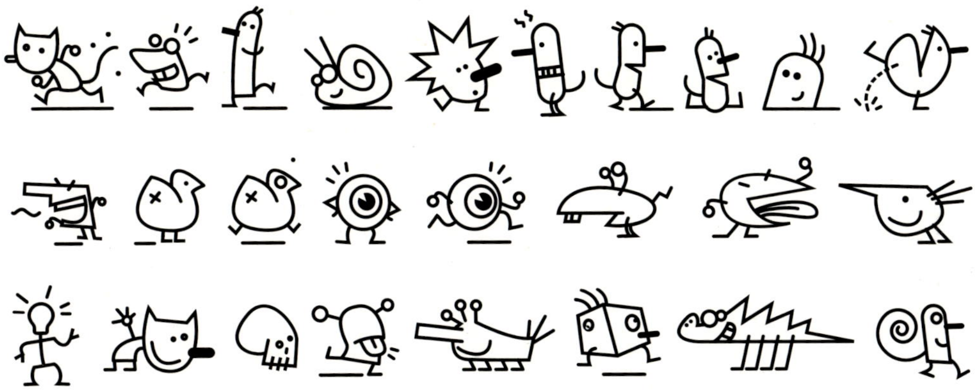

Chromosome	Dirk Uhlenbrock

the quick fox

abcdefghijkklmnopqrstuv

wxxyz0123456789[&:;!?@]

Cord Grob	Dirk Uhlenbrock

BROWN

ABCDEFGHIJ

KLMNOPQRS

TUVWXYZ01

23456789!

Gen3000 – Thin	Dirk Uhlenbrock

THE QUICK BROWN FOX JUMPS
BROWN FOX JUMPS OVER A LAZY DOG
ABCDEFGHIJKLMNOPQRSTUVWXYZ0123456789

Gen3000 – Regular	Dirk Uhlenbrock

THE QUICK BROWN FOX JUMPS
BROWN FOX JUMPS OVER A LAZY DOG
ABCDEFGHIJKLMNOPQRSTUVWXYZ0123456789

Ispy (selection)	Dirk Uhlenbrock

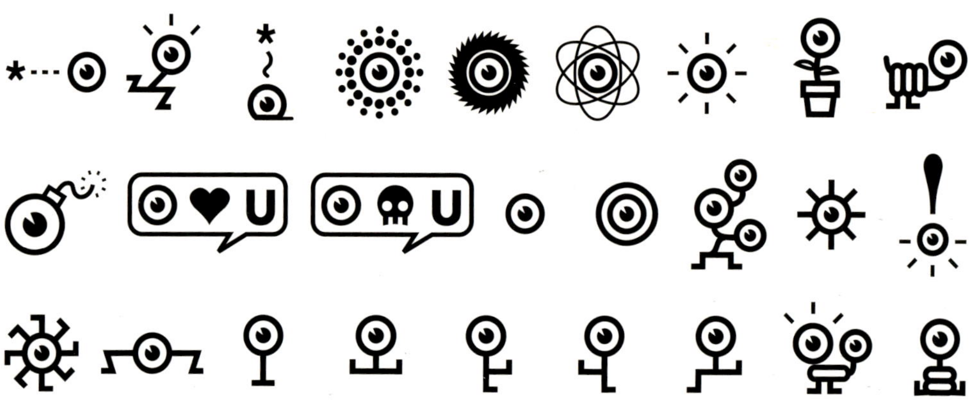

Hannelore – Regular | Dirk Uhlenbrock

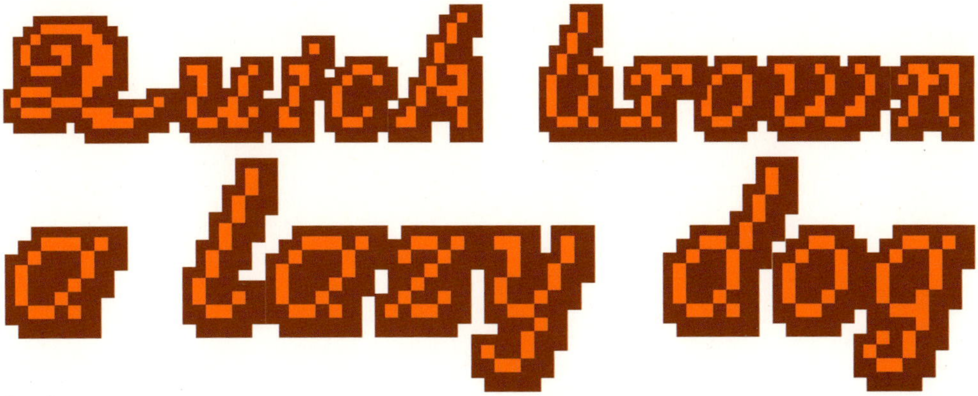

Regular

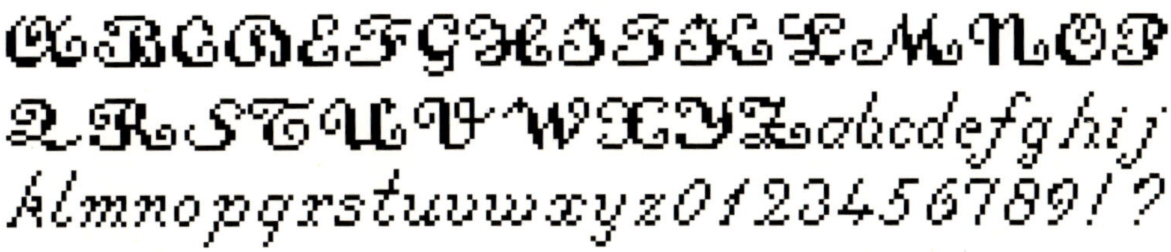

Outline

Jetset | Dirk Uhlenbrock

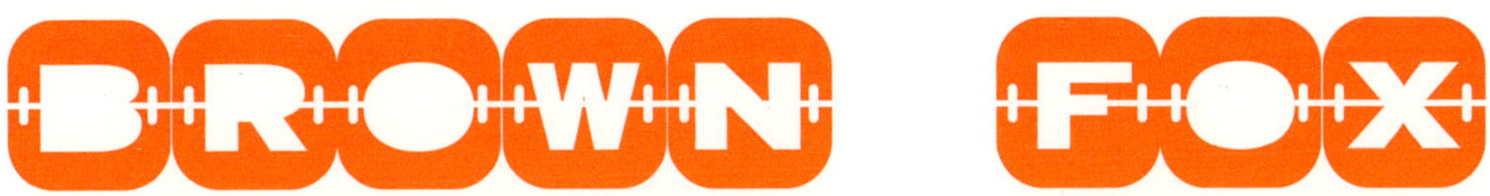

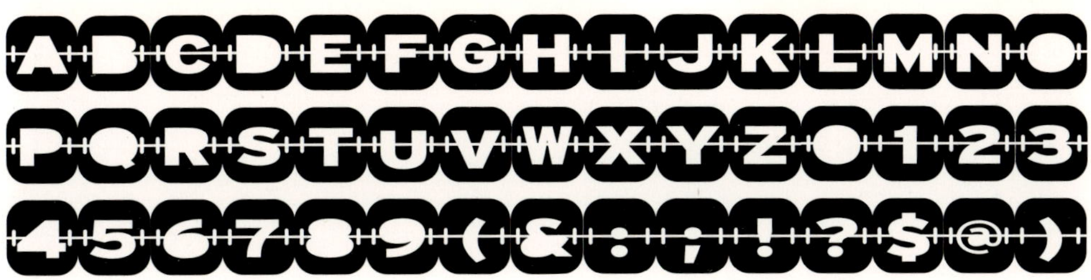

Honey | Dirk Uhlenbrock

THE QUICK BROWN

Light

ABCDEFGHIJKLMNOPQRSTUV
WXYZabcdefghijklmnopqr
stuvwxyz0123456789€!?$

Normal

ABCDEFGHIJKLMNOPQRSTUV
WXYZabcdefghijklmnopqr
stuvwxyz0123456789€!?$

Bold

ABCDEFGHIJKLMNOPQRSTUV
WXYZabcdefghijklmnopqr
stuvwxyz0123456789€!?$

Ultra

ABCDEFGHIJKLMNOPQRSTUV
WXYZabcdefghijklmnopqr
stuvwxyz0123456789€!?$

Mega – Thin | Dirk Uhlenbrock

THE FOX
JUMPS

AaBbCDdEeFGHhIJK
kLMnOPQRrSTtUVW
XYZ0123456789&$

Mega – Normal | Dirk Uhlenbrock

The brown
JUMPS

AaBbCDdEeFGHhIJK
kLMnOPQRrSTtUVW
XYZ0123456789&$

Mega – Bold | Dirk Uhlenbrock

FOX

AaBbCDdEeFGHhIJK
kLMnOPQRrSTtUVW
XYZ0123456789&$

Missu – Regular	Dirk Uhlenbrock

THE QUICK BROWN
LAZY DOG

ABCDEFGHIJKLMNOPQRSTU
VWXYZ0123456789[:;!?@]

Missu – Bold	Dirk Uhlenbrock

THE BROWN FOX
A LAZY DOG

ABCDEFGHIJKLMNOPQRSTU
VWXYZ0123456789[:;!?@]

Missu – Black	Dirk Uhlenbrock

THE QUICK BROWN
A LAZY DOG

ABCDEFGHIJKLMNOPQRSTU
VWXYZ0123456789[:;!?@]

THE QUICK
BROWN
FOX JUMPS
OVER
A LAZY DOG
ZWEI

Microbe	Dirk Uhlenbrock

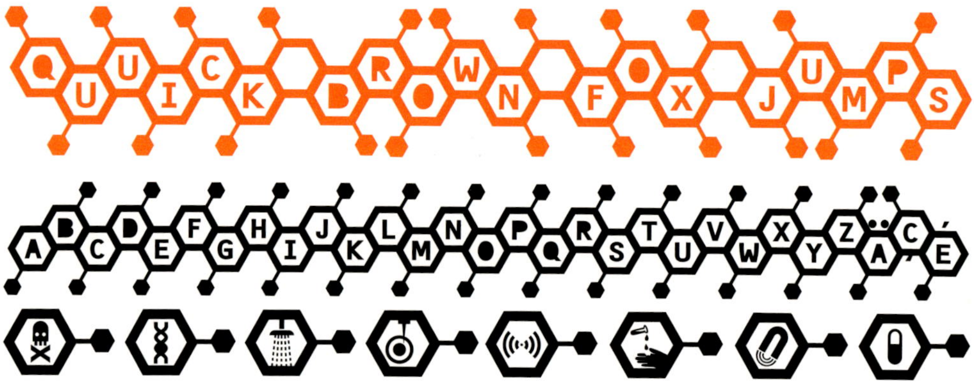

Ove – Thin	Dirk Uhlenbrock

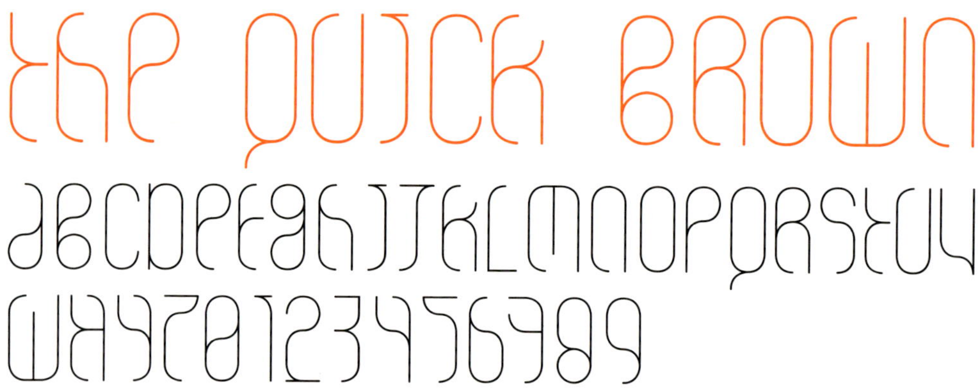

Ove – Regular	Dirk Uhlenbrock

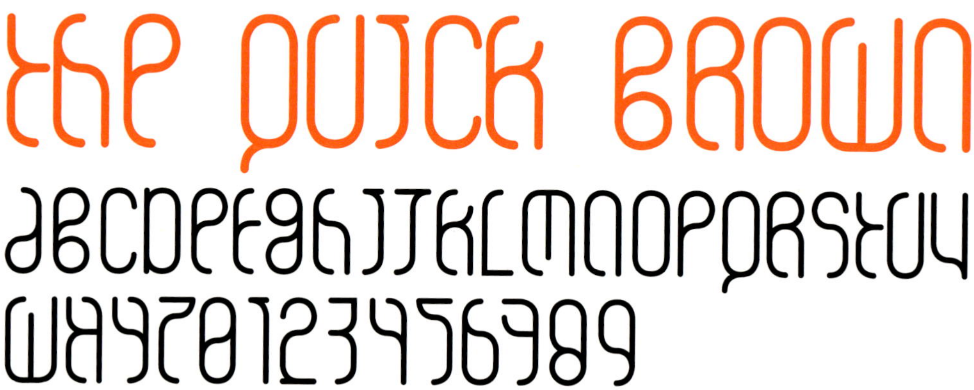

Pinx – Regular	Dirk Uhlenbrock

Quick brown fox

ABCDEFGHIJKLMNOPQRSTUVWXYZabcdefghij
klmnopqrstuvwxyz0123456789{&:;!?$@}

Pinx – Bold	Dirk Uhlenbrock

Quick brown fox

ABCDEFGHIJKLMNOPQRSTUVWXYZabcdefghij
klmnopqrstuvwxyz0123456789{&:;!?$@}

Pinx – Black	Dirk Uhlenbrock

Quick brown fox

ABCDEFGHIJKLMNOPQRSTUVWXYZabcdefghij
klmnopqrstuvwxyz0123456789{&:;!?$@}

Pellegrini – Regular | Dirk Uhlenbrock

Quick brown

ABCDEFGHIJKLMNOPQRSTUV
WHYZabcdefghijklmnopqrstu
vwxyz0123456789[&:;!?$¢€]

Pellegrini – Italic | Dirk Uhlenbrock

Quick lazy

ABCDEFGHIJKLMNOPQRSTUV
WHYZabcdefghijklmnopqrstu
vwxyz0123456789[&:;!?$¢€]

Rickshaw | Dirk Uhlenbrock

BROWN FOX JUMPS

ABCDEFGHIJKLMNOPQRSTUVWXYZAB
CDEFGHIJKLMNOPQRSTUVWXYZÅÇÉ≈

TypeType | typetype.net

Pile – Regular

Dirk Uhlenbrock

LAZY

ABCDEFGHIJKLMNO
PQRSTUVWXYZ0123
456789 ABCDEFGHIJKLM
NOPQRSTUVWXYZ0123456789

Pile – Outline

Dirk Uhlenbrock

A LAZY

ABCDEFGHIJKLMNO
PQRSTUVWXYZ0123
456789 ABCDEFGHIJKLM
NOPQRSTUVWXYZ0123456789

Thaiga – Thin

Dirk Uhlenbrock

the brown fox

abcdefghijklmnopqrstu
vwxyz0123456789(&:;!?@)

Thaiga – Thin Italic	Dirk Uhlenbrock

the brown fox
abcdefghijklmnopqrstu
vwxyz0123456789(&:;!?@)

Thaiga – Normal	Dirk Uhlenbrock

the brown fox
abcdefghijklmnopqrstu
vwxyz0123456789(&:;!?@)

Thaiga – Italic	Dirk Uhlenbrock

the brown fox
abcdefghijklmnopqrstu
vwxyz0123456789(&:;!?@)

Thaipe – Thin	Dirk Uhlenbrock

the brown fox

abcdefghijklmnopqrstu

vwxyz0123456789(&:;!?@)

Thaipe – Thin Italic	Dirk Uhlenbrock

the brown fox

abcdefghijklmnopqrstu

vwxyz0123456789(&:;!?@)

Thaipe – Normal	Dirk Uhlenbrock

the brown fox

abcdefghijklmnopqrstu

vwxyz0123456789(&:;!?@)

Thaipe – Italic	Dirk Uhlenbrock

the brown fox

abcdefghijklmnopqrstu

vwxyz0123456789(&:;!?@)

Treat	Dirk Uhlenbrock

THE QUICK
LAZY DOG

ABCDEFGHIJKLM

NOPQRSTUVWXYZ

0123456789&!?@

Tricky	Dirk Uhlenbrock

A LAZY

ABCDEFGHIJKLM

NOPQRSTUVWXYZ

0123456789&?$@

Quant – Light | Dirk Uhlenbrock

brown fox

ABCDEFGHIJKLMNOPQRSTUVW
XYZabcdefghijklmnopqrstuv
wxyz0123456789(&:;!?$@)

Quant – Regular | Dirk Uhlenbrock

Quick lazy

ABCDEFGHIJKLMNOPQRSTUVW
XYZabcdefghijklmnopqrstuv
wxyz0123456789(&:;!?$€@)

Quant – Bold | Dirk Uhlenbrock

Quick lazy

ABCDEFGHIJKLMNOPQRSTUVW
XYZabcdefghijklmnopqrstuv
wxyz0123456789(&:;!?$€@)

Toastheads (selection)	Dirk Uhlenbrock

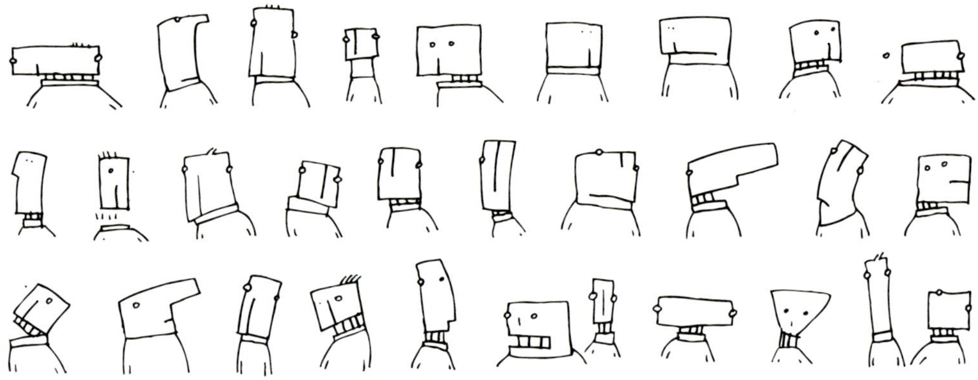

Turbon – Regular	Dirk Uhlenbrock

Over a lazy

ABCDEFGHIJKLMNOPQRSTUVW
XYZabcdefghijklmnopqrstũvwx
yzäçé0123456789&:;!?

Turbon – Italic	Dirk Uhlenbrock

Over lazy

ABCDEFGHIJKLMNOPQRSTUVW
XYZabcdefghijklmnopqrstũvwx
yzäçé0123456789&:;!?

Underware

underware.nl
info@underware.nl

Unibody 8 – Regular | Underware

ABCDEFGHIJKLMNOPQRSTUVWX
YZabcdefghijklmnopqrstuvw
xyzäçé0123456789(&:;!?$€)

THE QUICK BROWN FOX jumps over a lazy dog. Zwei Boxkämpfer jagen Eva quer durch Sylt. Lorem ipsum dolor sit amet, consectetur adipisicing elit, sed do eiusmod tempor incididunt ut labore et dolore magna aliqua. The quick brown fox jumps over a lazy dog. Zwei

Unibody 8 – Small Caps | Underware

ABCDEFGHIJKLMNOPQRSTUVWX
YZÄÇÉ0123456789
(&:;!?$¢£¥€@)

THE QUICK BROWN FOX JUMPS OVER A LAZY DOG. ZWEI BOXKÄMPFER JAGEN EVA QUER DURCH SYLT. LOREM IPSUM DOLOR SIT AMET, CONSECTETUR ADIPISICING ELIT, SED DO EIUSMOD TEMPOR INCIDIDUNT UT LABORE ET DOLORE MAGNA ALIQUA. THE QUICK BROWN FOX JUMPS OVER A LAZY DOG. ZWEI BOXKÄMPFER JAGEN EVA QUER DURCH SYLT. LOREM

Unibody 8 – Italic | Underware

ABCDEFGHIJKLMNOPQRSTUVWXYZ
abcdefghijklmnopqrstuvwxyzäçé
0123456789(&:;!?$¢£¥€@)

THE QUICK BROWN FOX jumps over a lazy dog. Zwei Boxkämpfer jagen Eva quer durch Sylt. Lorem ipsum dolor sit amet, consectetur adipisicing elit, sed do eiusmod tempor incididunt ut labore et dolore magna aliqua. The quick brown fox jumps over a lazy dog. Zwei Boxkämpfer jagen Eva quer

The quick
brown
fox jumps over
a lazy dog
ZWEI
Boxkämpfer

Underware | underware.nl

Unibody 8 – Bold	Underware

ABCDEFGHIJKLMNOPQRSTU
VWXYZabcdefghijklmnopq
rstuvwxyzäçé0123456789

THE QUICK BROWN FOX jumps over a lazy dog. Zwei Boxkämpfer jagen Eva quer durch Sylt. Lorem ipsum dolor sit amet, consectetur adipisicing elit, sed do eiusmod tempor incididunt ut labore et dolore magna aliqua. The quick brown

Unibody 8 – Black	Underware

ABCDEFGHIJKLMNOPQRS
TUVWXYZabcdefghijklmn
opqrstuvwxyz0123456789

THE QUICK BROWN FOX jumps over a lazy dog. Zwei Boxkämpfer jagen Eva quer durch Sylt. Lorem ipsum dolor sit amet, consectetur adipisicing elit, sed do eiusmod tempor incididunt ut labore et dolore magna aliqua. The quick brown vFive

vfive.com
roberto.christen@gmail.com

V5 Ampon – Upright	Roberto Christen

Brown Lazy

ABCDEFGHIJKLMNOPQRS
TUVWXYZabcdefghijkl
mnopqrstuvwxyzäçé
0123456789(&:;?$€£¥@)

V5 Ampon – Slanted	Roberto Christen

Brown Lazy

ABCDEFGHIJKLMNOPQRS
TUVWXYZabcdefghijkl
mnopqrstuvwxyzäçé
0123456789(&:;?$€£¥@)

V5 Ampon – Warped	Roberto Christen

Brown Lazy

ABCDEFGHIJKLMNOPQRS
TUVWXYZabcdefghijkl
mnopqrstuvwxyzäçé
0123456789(&:;?$€£¥@)

brown
lazy dog

Slim

abcdefghijklmno
pqrstuvwxyzäç
é0123456789!?$

Thick

abcdefghijklmno
pqrstuvwxyzäç
é0123456789!?$

Round

abcdefghijklmno
pqrstuvwxyzäç
é0123456789!?$

Outline

abcdefghijklmno
pqrstuvwxyzäç
é0123456789!?$

V5 Bloques | Roberto Christen

A☺LAZY

ABCDEFGHIJKLM

NOPQRSTUVWXYZ

0123456789&!?

V5 Eastergothic | Roberto Christen

THE LAZY DOG

ABCDEFGHIJKLMNOPQRSTUVWX

YZabcdefghijklmnopqrstuvwx

yzäçé0123456789(&:;!?$£¥€)

V5 Myopia | Roberto Christen

the quick brown fox

jumps over a

ABCDEFGHIJKLMNOPQRSTUVWXY

zabcdefghijklmnopqrstuvwx

yzäçé0123456789(&:;!?$£¥€@)

The quick brown fox jumps over a lazy dog zwei

V5 Loxica – Lixera	Roberto Christen

The quick brown fox jumps jumps over a lazy dog

ABCDEFGHIJKLMNOPQRSTUVWXYZabcdefg
hijklmnopqrstuvwxyzäçé0123456789&

V5 Loxica – Robusta	Roberto Christen

Quick brown

ABCDEFGHIJKLMNOPQRSTUVWXY
Zabcdefghijklmnopqrstuvwxy
zäçé0123456789(&:;!?$£¥€@)

V5 Pixelpals (selection)	Roberto Christen

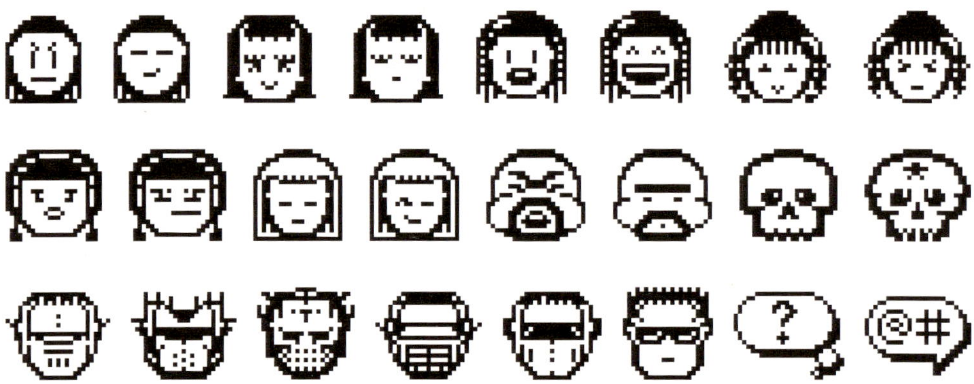

THE QUICK

Non

ABCDEFGHIJKLMNOPQR
STUVWXYZabcdefghij
klmnopqrstuvwxyzäç
é@0123456789(&.:;!?$¢€)

Dot

ABCDEFGHIJKLMNOPQR
STUVWXYZabcdefghij
klmnopqrstuvwxyzäç
é@0123456789(&.:;!?$¢€)

Cell

ABCDEFGHIJKLMNOPQR
STUVWXYZabcdefghij
klmnopqrstuvwxyzäç
é@0123456789(&.:;!?$¢€)

Fading

ABCDEFGHIJKLMNOPQR
STUVWXYZabcdefghij
klmnopqrstuvwxyzäç
é@0123456789(&.:;!?$¢€)

V5 Xtender | Roberto Christen

LAZY DOG

Regular

ABCDEFGHIJKLMNOPQR
STUVWXYZabcdefghij
klmnopqrstuvwxyzäç
é0123456789@[@!?$€]

Loin

ABCDEFGHIJKLMNOPQRS
tUVWXYZabcdefghijkl
mnopqrstuvwxyzäçé
0123456789@[@;!?$€@]

Loin Front

ABCDEFGHIJKLMNOPQRS
tUVWXYZabcdefghijkl
mnopqrstuvwxyzäçé
0123456789@[@;!?$€@]

Loin Back

ABCDEFGHIJKLMNOPQRS
tUVWXYZabcdefghijkl
mnopqrstuvwxyzäçé
0123456789@[@;!?$€@]

Wojciech Kalinowski

wmk69@o2.pl

Classica – Book	Wojciech Kalinowski

QUICK FOX

ABCDEFGHIJKLMNOPQRSTUVW
XYZabcdefghijklmnopqrstuvw
xyząçě0123456789(&:;!?$£¥€)

Classica – Bold	Wojciech Kalinowski

FOX OVER

ABCDEFGHIJKLMNOPQRSTU
VWXYZabcdefghijklmnopq
rstuvwxyząçě0123456789&

Gothica – Book	Wojciech Kalinowski

Quick brown

ABCDEFGHIJKLMNOPQRSTUVW
XYZabcdefghijklmnopqrstuvwx
yząçě0123456789(&:;!?$¢£¥€)

Gothica – Bold	Wojciech Kalinowski

Brown lazy

ABCDEFGHIJKLMNOPQRSTU
UWXYZabcdefghijklmnopqr
stuuwxyzżąçě0123456789&

Consola Mono	Wojciech Kalinowski

ABCDEFGHIJKLMNOPQRSTUVWXY
Zabcdefghijklmnopqrstuvwx
yząçě0123456789(&!?$¢£¥€)
АБВГДЕЁЖЗИЙКЛМНОПРСТУФХЦЧ
ШЩЪЫЬЭЮЯабвгдеёжзийклмноп
рстуфхцчшщъыьэюя
ΑΒΓΔΕΖΗΘΙΚΛΜΝΞΟΠΡΣΤΥΦΧΨΩ
αβγδεζηθικλμνξοπρσςτυφχψω

THE QUICK BROWN FOX jumps over a lazy dog. Zwei Boxkämpfer jagen Eva quer durch Sylt. Lorem ipsum dolor sit amet, consectetur adipisicing elit, sed do eiusmod tempor incididunt ut labore et dolore magna aliqua. The quick brown fox jumps over a lazy dog. Zwei Boxkämpfer jagen Eva quer durch Sylt. Lorem ipsum dolor sit amet, consecte-

Cursive Sans	Wojciech Kalinowski

Quick brown

ABCDEFGHIJKLMNOPQRSTUV
WXYZabcdefghijklmnopqrstu
vwxyząçě0123456789(&;:!?€)

Cursive Serif	Wojciech Kalinowski

Quick brown

ABCDEFGHIJKLMNOPQRSTUV
WXYZabcdefghijklmnopqrstu
vwxyząçě0123456789(&;:!?€)

Modern Antiqua	Wojciech Kalinowski

Quick brown

ABCDEFGHIJKLMNOPQRSTUV
WXYZabcdefghijklmnopqrstu
vwxyząçě0123456789(&;:!?€)

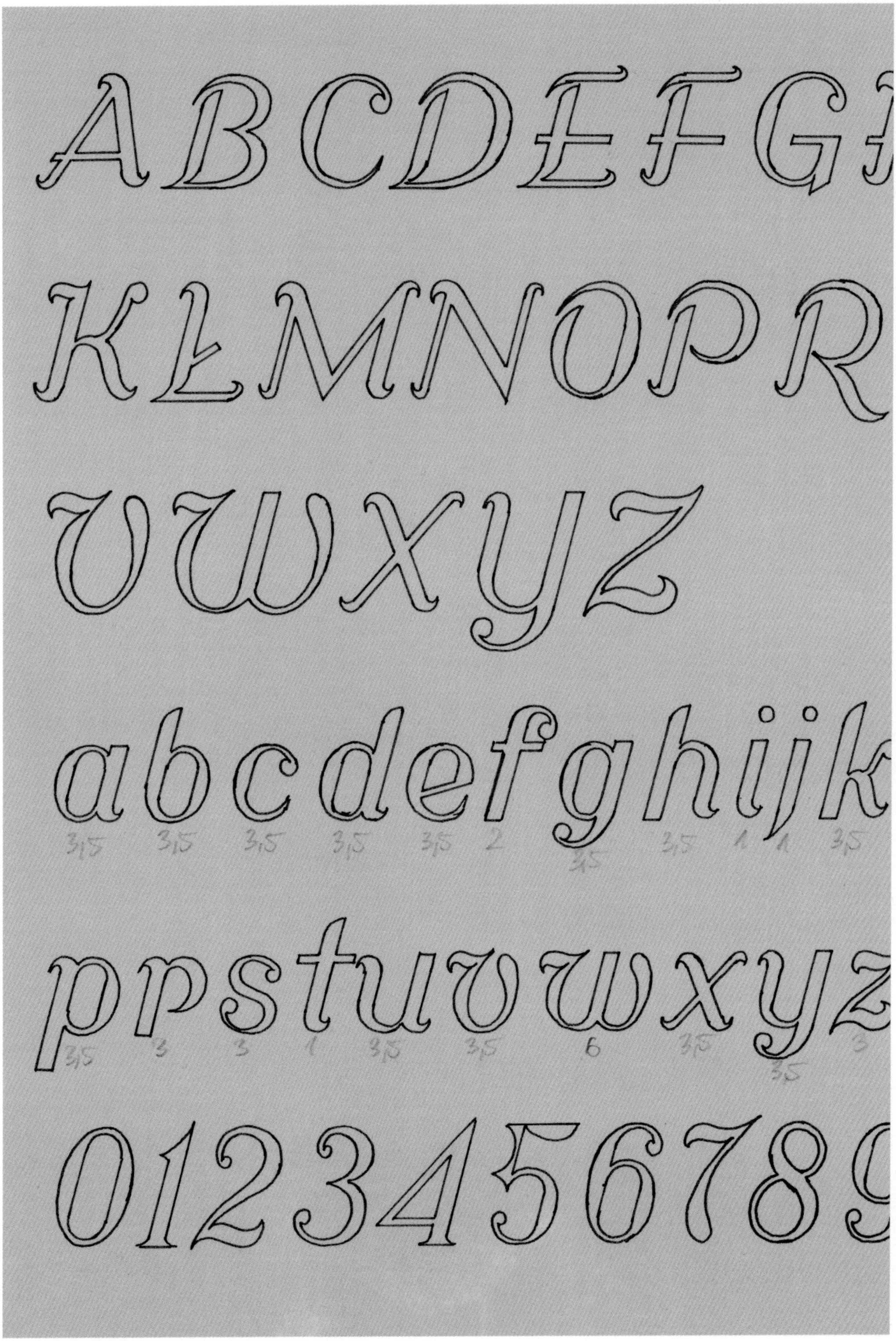

Drawings for the typeface Cursive Serif. © 2012 Wojciech Kalinowski

Berenika – Book	Wojciech Kalinowski

Brown fox

ABCDEFGHIJKLMNOPQRSTU
VWXYZabcdefghijklmnopqrst
uvwxyząçĕ0123456789(&:;!?)

Berenika – Oblique	Wojciech Kalinowski

Brown fox

ABCDEFGHIJKLMNOPQRSTU
VWXYZabcdefghijklmnopqrst
uvwxyząçĕ0123456789(&:;!?)

Berenika – Bold	Wojciech Kalinowski

Quick fox

ABCDEFGHIJKLMNOPQRS
TUVWXYZabcdefghijklmno
pqrstuvwxyząçĕ01234567

Berenika – Bold Oblique	Wojciech Kalinowski

Quick fox

ABCDEFGHIJKLMNOPQRS
TUVWXYZabcdefghijklmno
pqrstuvwxyząçĕ01234567

Klaudia – Book	Wojciech Kalinowski

Brown fox

ABCDEFGHIJKLMNOPQRSTU
VWXYZabcdefghijklmnopqrst
uvwxyząçĕ0123456789(&:;!?)

Klaudia – Oblique	Wojciech Kalinowski

Brown fox

ABCDEFGHIJKLMNOPQRSTU
VWXYZabcdefghijklmnopqrst
uvwxyząçĕ0123456789(&:;!?)

Klaudia – Bold	Wojciech Kalinowski

Quick fox

ABCDEFGHIJKLMNOPQRS
TUVWXYZabcdefghijklmno
pqrstuvwxyząçě01234567

Klaudia – Bold Oblique	Wojciech Kalinowski

Quick fox

ABCDEFGHIJKLMNOPQRS
TUVWXYZabcdefghijklmno
pqrstuvwxyząçě01234567

Medieval Sharp – Book	Wojciech Kalinowski

The quick fox

ABCDEFGHIJKLMNOPQRSTUVW
XYZabcdefghijklmnopqrstuvwx
yząçě0123456789(&;:!?$¢£¥€)

Medieval Sharp – Oblique	Wojciech Kalinowski

The quick fox

ABCDEFGHIJKLMNOPQRSTUVW
XYZabcdefghijklmnopqrstuvwx
yząçě0123456789(&;:!?$¢£¥€)

Medieval Sharp – Bold	Wojciech Kalinowski

Brown lazy

ABCDEFGHIJKLMNOPQRSTU
VWXYZabcdefghijklmnopqr
stuvwxyząçě0123456789!?

Medieval Sharp – Bold Oblique	Wojciech Kalinowski

Brown lazy

ABCDEFGHIJKLMNOPQRSTU
VWXYZabcdefghijklmnopqr
stuvwxyząçě0123456789!?

Nova Cut	Wojciech Kalinowski

Quick brown

ABCDEFGHIJKLMNOPQRSTUV
WXYZabcdefghijklmnopqrstuv
wxyząçě0123456789(&:;!?€)

Nova Flat	Wojciech Kalinowski

Quick brown

ABCDEFGHIJKLMNOPQRSTUV
WXYZabcdefghijklmnopqrstuv
wxyząçě0123456789(&:;!?€)

Nova Oval	Wojciech Kalinowski

Quick brown

ABCDEFGHIJKLMNOPQRSTUV
WXYZabcdefghijklmnopqrstuv
wxyząçě0123456789(&:;!?$€)

Nova Round	Wojciech Kalinowski

Quick brown

ABCDEFGHIJKLMNOPQRSTUV
WXYZabcdefghijklmnopqrstuv
wxyząçě0123456789(&:;!?€)

Nova Script	Wojciech Kalinowski

Quick brown

ABCDEFGHIJKLMNOPQRSTUV
WXYZabcdefghijklmnopqrstuv
wxyząçě0123456789(&:;!?$€)

Nova Slim	Wojciech Kalinowski

Quick brown

ABCDEFGHIJKLMNOPQRSTUV
WXYZabcdefghijklmnopqrstuv
wxyząçě0123456789(&:;!?€)

Nova Square	Wojciech Kalinowski

Quick brown

ABCDEFGHIJKLMNOPQRSTUV
WXYZabcdefghijklmnopqrstuv
wxyząçě0123456789(&:;!?€)

Round Style Basic	Wojciech Kalinowski

Quick brown

ABCDEFGHIJKLMNOPQRST
UVWXYZabcdefghijklmnopq
rstuvwxyząçě0123456789$

Round Style Deco	Wojciech Kalinowski

Quick brown

ABCDEFGHIJKLMNOPQRST
UVWXYZabcdefghijklmnopq
rstuvwxyząçě0123456789$

Round Style Middle	Wojciech Kalinowski

Quick brown

ABCDEFGHIJKLMNOPQRST
UVWXYZabcdefghijklmnopq
rstuvwxyząçě0123456789$

Round Style Simple	Wojciech Kalinowski

Quick brown

ABCDEFGHIJKLMNOPQRST
UVWXYZabcdefghijklmnopq
rstuvwxyząçě0123456789$

Square Antiqua – Book	Wojciech Kalinowski

Quick brown

ABCDEFGHIJKLMNOPQRSTUVW
XYZabcdefghijklmnopqrstuvw
xyząçě0123456789(&:;!?$£€)

Square Antiqua – Oblique	Wojciech Kalinowski

Quick brown

*ABCDEFGHIJKLMNOPQRSTUVW
XYZabcdefghijklmnopqrstuvw
xyząçě0123456789(&:;!?$£€)*

Square Antiqua – Bold	Wojciech Kalinowski

Brown lazy

**ABCDEFGHIJKLMNOPQRSTU
VWXYZabcdefghijklmnopqr
stuvwxyząçě0123456789€**

Square Antiqua – Bold Oblique	Wojciech Kalinowski

Brown lazy

***ABCDEFGHIJKLMNOPQRSTU
VWXYZabcdefghijklmnopqr
stuvwxyząçě0123456789€***

Character sets

As is the nature of free fonts, the character sets of the fonts included in this book are not uniform. Most (but not all) of the fonts contain at least a full set of upper and lower case letters and numbers; many contain accented characters used in Western European languages. Some of the fonts contain extended character sets, including Central and Eastern European, Cyrillic and/or Greek.

Although OpenType fonts on the CD are suitable for both Windows and Mac, they might contain special characters that can only be accessed with the help of software that supports OpenType features.

CD and font licensing

The free fonts included on the CD accompanying this book are licensed by their respective designers/foundries for use solely by the owner of this book. Although all free fonts included with this book are licensed for personal and commercial use, you may only use the fonts in accordance with the terms set forth in the respective End User Licence Agreements (EULAs). Please consult the appropriate EULA and/or 'read me' files, included with each font on the CD, before using any font.

The Pepin Press, the author and the designers/foundries are not liable for any damage resulting from the use of the CD, font software or any accompanying documentation. Please contact the individual designers/foundries for additional information on licensing.

Please consult the documentation that came with your system and/or software for information on how to install fonts on your computer. You can also contact the designer/foundry or check one of the many resources available on the internet.

Zeichensätze

Da es sich in diesem Buch um Free Fonts handelt, sind die Zeichensätze der hier vorgestellten Schriften natürlich nicht einheitlich. Die meisten (wenn auch nicht alle) Schriften enthalten zumindest vollständige Sätze von Majuskeln, Minuskeln und Ziffern, und viele auch Akzentbuchstaben, wie sie in westeuropäischen Sprachen gebraucht werden. Einige der Schriften haben erweiterte Zeichensätze mit mittel- und osteuropäischen, kyrillischen bzw. griechischen Zeichen.

Die OpenType-Schriften von der CD sind sowohl für Windows als auch Mac geeignet, enthalten aber ggf. Sonderzeichen, auf die man nur mit Software zugreifen kann, die OpenType-Eigenschaften unterstützt.

CD und Schriftlizenzierung

Die Free Fonts auf der beiliegenden CD sind von ihren Designern/Herstellern ausschließlich für den Gebrauch durch den Eigentümer dieses Buches lizenziert. Obwohl alle Free Fonts, die diesem Buch beiliegen, für privaten und kommerziellen Gebrauch lizenziert sind, dürfen Sie die Fonts nur zu den in der betreffenden Endbenutzer-Lizenzvereinbarung (EULA) festgelegten Bedingungen verwenden. Bitte ziehen Sie die betreffende EULA (in englischer Sprache) und/oder die Readme-Dateien heran, die jeder Schrift auf der CD beiliegt, bevor Sie einen Font verwenden.

The Pepin Press, der Autor und die Schriftdesigner/-hersteller haften nicht für Schäden durch Verwendung der CD, der Fontsoftware oder der beiliegenden Dokumentation. Bitte kontaktieren Sie die einzelnen Schriftdesigner/-herausgeber für weitere Informationen zur Lizenzierung.

Ziehen Sie zur Installation von Fonts auf Ihrem Computer die Dokumentation heran, die Sie mit Ihrer Hard- oder Software erhalten haben. Sie können auch die Schriftdesigner/-hersteller kontaktieren oder eine der zahlreichen Online-Ressourcen im Internet konsultieren.

Jeux de caractères

De par la nature même des typographies libres, les jeux de caractères des polices présentées dans ce livre ne sont pas toutes uniformes. La plupart des fontes (mais pas toutes) possèdent au moins un jeu complet de lettres capitales, de minuscules et de chiffres. Beaucoup possèdent les caractères accentués utilisés dans les langues d'Europe occidentale. Certaines typographies possèdent des jeux de caractères additionnels, incluant les caractères des langues d'Europe centrale et orientale ainsi que les caractères cyrilliques et/ou grecs.

Bien que les typographies au format OpenType, figurant sur le CD, sont compatibles à la fois avec les systèmes Windows et Mac, elles peuvent cependant posséder des caractères spéciaux qui ne peuvent être visualisés sans l'aide d'un logiciel supportant les caractéristiques OpenType.

Contrat de licence concernant le CD et les typographies

Les typographies libres, contenues dans le CD accompagnant le livre, font l'objet d'une licence de la part de leur créateur ou fonderie respectif qui restreint leur utilisation au propriétaire de ce livre exclusivement. Bien que toutes les fontes libres fournies avec ce livre bénéficient d'une licence pour usage personnel et commercial, leur utilisation doit respecter les conditions stipulées dans les contrats de licence d'utilisateur final (CLU) respectifs. Avant d'utiliser une typographie, veuillez consulter le CLU (en anglais) et/ou le fichier « read-me » (lisez-moi) accompagnant chaque fonte contenue sur le CD.

L'éditeur The Pepin Press, l'auteur et les créateurs de typographie ne peuvent être tenus responsables des dommages pouvant résulter de l'utilisation du CD, du logiciel de fontes ou de la documentation qui les accompagne. Pour de plus amples informations sur les licences, veuillez contacter les typographes ou les fonderies respectives.

Pour plus d'informations sur la façon d'installer des polices sur votre ordinateur, veuillez vous reportez à la documentation fournie avec votre système et/ou logiciel. Vous pouvez également contacter le créateur ou la fonderie ou consulter une des nombreuses ressources disponibles sur internet.

Series tipográficas

En línea con la naturaleza de las tipografías gratuitas, las familias tipográficas recopiladas en esta obra son heterogéneas. La mayoría de ellas (si bien no todas) contienen, como mínimo, una serie completa de letras en caja alta y baja, y números; además muchas incluyen caracteres con tilde empleados por las lenguas europeas occidentales. Algunas tipografías incluyen series tipográficas ampliadas, entre las que se cuentan las correspondientes a Europa central y oriental, cirílico o griego.

Aunque las tipografías OpenType del CD son compatibles con Windows y Mac, es posible que contengan caracteres especiales que solo son accesibles con software especializado que soporte las características OpenType.

CD y licencias de uso de las tipografías

Las tipografías gratuitas incluidas en el CD adjunto son propiedad de sus respectivos diseñadores/fundiciones y se licencian para uso exclusivo del propietario de este libro. Pese a que todas las fuentes gratuitas incluidas en este volumen se ceden con licencia tanto para uso personal como comercial, deben usarse con acuerdo a los términos y condiciones establecidos en los contratos de licencia para usuarios finales (EULA) correspondientes. Consulte el EULA (en Inglés) pertinente y/o los archivos «read me» (léame) incluidos con cada tipografía en el CD adjunto antes de utilizarla.

The Pepin Press, el autor y los diseñadores tipográficos quedan exentos de toda responsabilidad por cualquier posible daño derivado del uso del CD, el *software* de creación tipográfica o la documentación adjunta. Contacte con los diseñadores o las fundiciones correspondientes si precisa información adicional acerca de los términos de la licencia.

Para obtener información sobre cómo instalar tipografías en su ordenador, consulte la documentación provista con su equipo o *software*. Asimismo, puede ponerse en contacto con el diseñador / fundición o consultar alguna de las numerosas fuentes disponibles en la red.

About the authors

Hans Lijklema is a graphic design graduate of the Minerva school of fine arts in Groningen, the Netherlands. Since 1996 he has been living in Warsaw, Poland, where he worked as a senior graphic designer at Saatchi & Saatchi and later became the design director of Saatchi & Saatchi Design. Since 2001 Hans Lijklema has run his own design practice, Lijklema Design, together with Karolina Lijklema – a graduate of the poster design atelier of Prof. M. Wasilewski, at the Warsaw Academy of Fine Arts. Over the years they have designed mainly book covers, corporate identities and packaging for local as well as international clients. Their book cover designs have been nominated by the Polish Book Publishers' Association for the 'Most Beautiful Book of the Year' award.
Hans and Karolina Lijklema are the authors of various books on graphic design and illustration as well as several children's books.

lijklema.waw.pl

Other Pepin Press books by the same authors:

Free Font Index 1
ISBN 978 90 5768 124 0

Free Font Index 2
ISBN 978 90 5768 147 9

Pictographic Index 1
ISBN 978 90 5768 134 9

Pictographic Index 2: Design for Music
ISBN 978 90 5768 157 8